After Materialism — What?

AFTER MATERIALISM— WHAT?

by

SIR RICHARD CLIFFORD TUTE

ANDREW MELROSE LTD

London   New York   Melbourne   Sydney   Cape Town

Made and Printed in Great Britain by
GREYCAINES
*(Taylor Garnett Evans & Co. Ltd.)
Watford, Herts.*

CONTENTS

". . . we have no right to assume that this external world is . . . itself confined within the limits of space and time . . . we must move to some new plane of thought before we can realize that the particles and the waves are shadow pictures of one and the same universe."

Sir James Jeans in *Man and the Universe* being the first chapter in a book entitled *Scientific Progress* (Macmillan).

AUTHOR'S PREFACE

THE first chapter of this book is its proper preface. It was written to elicit the views of men of science as to the extent to which modern developments of knowledge operate to modify the nineteenth century attitude towards religion. As the invitation was not taken up, and as I felt strongly that someone ought to make a beginning in discussing this important matter, I proceeded with trepidation to attempt the work myself. I have made the necessary apologies for trespassing on a realm that lies outside my specialized training in the second chapter, and will not repeat them here.

The decay of the Christian religion has been a commonplace of discussion in scientific circles for perhaps a century and a half. During the last half of the nineteenth century this form of discussion gave rise to a flood of literature which tended to bring religion in general, and particularly the Christian religion into contempt, as being a phase in the evolution of man which is in course of being eliminated by the spread of truer knowledge.

As a result Christianity has suffered a notable eclipse. But, this development, which was so recently and so earnestly desired as an emancipation by its opponents, has not operated as an emancipation. Where it has been complete, as in Russia, it has brought about a universal regimentation of the body and the mind alike. In Germany it gave rise to a new paganism accompanied by a new barbarism more complete than any that the world has witnessed. In Italy political conditions, largely due to the presence of the Papacy in Rome prevented the extremes presented by Russia and Germany from attaining full development. In other countries there has been a notable decay of religious observance, and with it an increase of crime and careless living. As a result the power of these countries to resist attack, alike from within and from without, was notably weakened. Of these conditions Germany took ruthless advantage.

We can now see, what the philosophers and scientists of the last century failed to see, that the democracy which we are so desperately defending is itself a Christian product. The Christian religion is the only religion which proclaims, and in practice maintains, the brotherhood of men. It is on belief in that Christian doctrine that democracy rests. Manhood's suffrage has no other basis. It follows that Christianity and democracy must sink or swim together. The spiritual faith must revive, if the correlated political system is to survive.

From this point of view it is incumbent on everyone who believes that he has a contribution to make towards religious revival to make it.

Considered from the side of religion, the importance of scientific theories, like the theory of relativity in its various stages, and the quantic theories, lies, not so much in the additions they make to our knowledge, as in the extent to which they limit the possibilities of knowledge. Reality for the physicist was formerly what he could perceive, or might with proper apparatus perceive. It stretched away into infinite space, and endured through infinite time. It was a prison for the soul of infinite extent, and few possibilities. This attitude has disappeared. Reality is now what we do not perceive. It is infinitely greater than what is or can be perceived, and has infinite spiritual as well as material possibilities.

It is this immense extension of the physical and spiritual fields alike that is of interest to the believer as well as to the scientist.

However, I will not here continue to discuss matters which are more fully dealt with in the body of the book. I will merely remark that the new concept of reality virtually coincides with the content of the mystic experience in the forms in which it has been reached by philosophers like Plato and Plotinus, by some of the Christian mystics, and by the Hindu Yogis. That experience shows that in all ages, and many countries, men have actually penetrated to a super sensual reality, which must be identified with the new scientific background. They have, in other words, penetrated to the home of the spirit, and found it to be a scientific fact.

I cannot find that any modern philosopher, with the single exception of P. D. Ouspensky, has seen this remarkable connection. Unfortunately, he has oriented himself in the direction of Hindu philosophy, and is, therefore, only partially available for purely Christian defence. He has found a truth, but it is a secondary truth; and it is not the truth of which the world stands in need to-day. Other philosophic scientists, such as Sir Arthur Eddington, Professor A. N. Whitehead, and Sir James Jeans, have grasped the mystery, but not the mystic connection. At any rate if they have grasped it they have not said so. They are on the side of religion, but they have not realized that religion, every religion, is based on mysticism. They have failed, in other words, to avail themselves of more than a part of the evidence, and in doing so they have failed to see certain aspects of mysticism, which are of great value to their own researches as physicists. These matters will be dealt with in due course.

Acknowledgments are due to Dr. L. P. Jacks, the editor of the *Hibbert Journal* in which the first three chapters of this book originally appeared. I have been greatly helped in the arrangement of the manuscript for publication by Mr. Frank L. Baer.

CHAPTER I

AFTER MATERIALISM—WHAT?

DR. CARREL has insisted on the dangers of a materialistic philosophy to nations and individuals alike. His great book, *Man the Unknown*, deals mainly with conditions in the United States; but the lessons that he draws from those conditions are applicable throughout the civilized world. Materialism is a view of life which regards man as a product, actually a by-product, of a mechanistic universe. His importance in the scheme of things is negligible. The planet on which he lives is a speck in the sum of things. The universe is the product of blind forces operating through æons of time on dead matter.

Matter obeys laws, called the laws of Nature, and, because it does so, the result of their operation has been a scheme which is not chaotic. In course of time life appeared in rudimentary forms as a product of matter and the forces operating on it. The first simple forms gradually became complex.

Under the stress of forces as blind as those which produced the stars, the chief of which was a cruel process called the struggle for existence, man appeared in succession to a line of simian forbears. He lived in simple societies which became increasingly complex. His fears, superstitions, and primitive rites followed a parallel course, and finally evolved into the religions which are in existence to-day. The morality imposed by those religions has no sanction more binding than the habits which evolution has imposed on the social animals and insects. Nothing exists that can be called supernatural.

Though we do not know how life arose from dead matter, we may be certain that, as the scope of science expands, an explanation will be found. Consciousness appears to be an epiphenomenon, a by-product of the blind forces which made the universe.

Finally, as all things are the result of the operation of the laws of Nature on dead matter, the chain of causation remains unbroken as much in living things as in dead. It follows that man is mistaken in supposing himself to be a free agent.

Such, in brief, is the account given by the materialist of the universe in which we live and of our own being.

It came to its full development in the last century as a result of the great increase of knowledge which that century witnessed. Under its influence, which is still widespread, religion has been widely discredited. Private and public morality have at the same time degenerated under the influence of teaching which denies to every system of morals any supernatural value. The existence of a God who created the universe has either been denied outright, as in Russia, or else regarded as an unimportant, because unmeaning, factor in a universe which is wholly mechanical.

The scientists under whose influence this view arose were honest seekers after truth. They observed a high standard of integrity in their work, and may be said to have substituted the worship of scientific truth for religion. Their ideal was a high one; and, as all high ideals which are honestly entertained have enormous power, their doctrines spread over the world until they found their final flowering in social theories like those of Karl Marx, and in a professedly atheistic government like that of Russia.

In all countries which can claim to be civilized, materialism has exercised enormous influence. It teaches men that they are no better than the beasts of the field, and men are responding to that teaching by behaving as beasts to an extent which the scientists and philosophers of the last century hardly contemplated.

In Russia the denial of religion has itself become a religion. In the United States, if Dr. Carrel is to be believed, the doctrines of materialism are responsible for widespread mental and moral deterioration and for the encouragement of a dogmatic attitude of mind, which is doing great harm in the biological, medical, and social sciences.

As already indicated, it is not surprising that men who believe themselves to be no better than the beasts should act amorally. In the realm of science of the types indicated the influence of materialism is seen (*inter alia*) in a reluctance to recognize man as a complex being, whose consciousness and mental activities are as important and as real as his body.

Instead of treating him as a whole—a conscious whole —they find it more in accordance with doctrines, which regard mental phenomena as less real than the physical, to treat him as an aggregate of separate organs. The procedure leads to specialization by practitioners, who never acquire the knowledge needed to follow the operations of the organ in which they have specialized beyond its material frontiers. It leads to a neglect of the action of mind on body and of body on mind.

The triumphs of medicine and hygiene, which have robbed many of the great diseases of their terrors, are largely offset by an increase of lunacy and mental and nervous disorders. The improvement of the national physique, due to the new methods of education and upbringing, appears to be correlated with a lack of courage, imagination, and stamina.

In short, methods of treating man which rest themselves on his worldly needs and physical make-up have not justified themselves.

I have mentioned these matters as an introduction to a subject with which Dr. Carrel has not expressly dealt, but which constitutes and important indictment of materialism. I refer to the fact, now acknowledged by scientific men, that the science on which materialism is based is no longer recognized as true. Matter and the laws of Nature, which were supposed to control it, are not in the least what the materialist assumed them to be.

Our modern view of the universe is based on mystical conceptions which he repudiates as savouring of superstition and charlatanry. Our reason is now known to be limited by the structure of our minds, and cannot deal effectively with more than a fraction of our experiences. The remainder is knowledge which is incommensurable, and therefore out of the reach of the method of science. Space and time are the factors which give form to our preceptions; but space and time are forms of thought, and not forms of things.

What things are in themselves is beyond all knowledge, and must be forever beyond it. Reality is a concept which has no meaning in the sense contemplated by the materialist. Nothing in this life is real except the passing show, the universal film in which we are actors, the scene which keeps changing as long as life endures, as the great Operator (whoever He may be) passes the roll of film before the light of our conscious life.

It is strange but true that these facts—they are facts and not ravings—are never faced by the materialist. Materialism, or at any rate an outlook on life which assumes the truth of materialism, is the doctrine in which most of the youth of the present day are being brought up. Its teachings are supposed to be the necessary basis of the scientific outlook, and of scientific method. Their justification is supposed to be exhibited in the triumphs which science has achieved in every department of research, and in practically every activity of our lives.

There is a truth in this contention; but it is only a part of the truth, and, as Dr. Carrel has indicated, it has its dangers. If the pursuit of science is regarded as the most important thing in life, and its results, in the form of health and comfort, as the be all and end all of existence, then an untrue philosophy might be tolerated.

But experience is showing that it is dangerous alike to the individual and to his civilization to take this view. For the individual it spells degeneration. For the State it means —what we saw in Germany and Japan. The degenerate individual is not happy; and there are few who will assert that happiness is an outstanding feature of life in the countries mentioned.

A brief account of some of the findings of modern science

is required to show that our indictment of materialism is to be taken seriously.

Before giving it I would like to point out that I do not assume that materialists are generally ignorant of those findings. What I do assert is that to remain materialists they must have failed to appreciate what they imply. They are not merely additions to pre-existing knowledge. They are denials that that knowledge can any longer claim to be knowledge. When Rutherford split the atom he exploded the philosophy which was based on the old conception of the atom.

Well, as to the atom in question. What the old materialism regarded as the smallest portion into which matter can be divided either by experiment or in imagination, and which is itself composed in its entirety of a single element, has now been shown to be more like a dance of points of negative energy round a point of positive energy in a void, which constitutes by far the greater portion of its bulk.

On this view the atom has been likened to a planetary system in miniature. As disembodied energy is not matter, and as void is not matter in any sense which can be assigned to that much abused term, it follows that the atom is immaterial. In other words, it is a mystery. It represents a dead end beyond which knowledge, reasoned knowledge, cannot go. We can say if we like, and it has been said in responsible quarters, that it may be a mental phenomenon. In other words, it may be the thought of some Being.

Later research has disclosed that the make-up of the atom cannot be described as simply as the planetary scheme indicates. Scientists are now at work to describe its constitution and activities by means of wave and probability theories, which involve mathematics of an intensely ideal kind. The operations in question are such as cannot be pictured by the intelligence and must seek justification in their results. The process is intuitional rather than reasonable.

It is evident that so long as we could suppose that we know what matter is, we were justified in explaining other things in terms of matter. But as we must now abandon that position, we must abandon with it the possibility of using it as the starting point of further explanation. I do not mean to say that, because we don't know the constitution of the atom in any but a metaphysical sense, we must halt all chemical and physical research till we can better our knowledge of it. That is not intended. What is intended is to indicate that it can no longer be used as an ultimate explanation of the universe. We cannot use it to support a philosophy. The universe meanwhile continues to exist unexplained on the basis of what matter appears to be, and must so continue to exist. This is the first argument against the old materialism. It has no solid root.

The next consideration depends on the theory of relativity, which has replaced the theory, or rather the assumption, as to the nature of human knowledge on which materialism rests. That assumption is that external things are like what our minds picture them to be. The world is very much as we see it. This notion has now been blown kite high. The story is not perhaps as well known as it might be. At any rate a short account of what has happened will clear the way for later discussion.

It was supposed that light is propagated by means of waves. As waves imply something in which they occur, the old scientists assumed the existence of an ether which would perform this function. Experiments were undertaken to find out the rate of the progress of our planet through this ether. They consisted in measuring the speed of light in all directions. It was found that speed is a constant quantity in every direction. It is the same whether we are approaching or leaving the source of the light. It is the same whether the source is leaving or approaching us. The ether was not found at all.

Other experiments, this time with electrical aggregates, showed that the said aggregates shorten in the direction of a motion that has been imparted to them. Incidentally, the new view of the atom shows it to be an electrical aggregate, and also that the earth itself, being an aggregate of atoms, is such an aggregate.

On combining the two results it was found that they satisfied and indeed necessitated an equation which revolutionizes our ideas about human knowledge. It shows that what had hitherto been taken as the distance between two points is really a quantity dependent on time as well as space. For the speeds dealt with in ordinary life the intrusion of the time element is not ordinarily noticeable; but at speeds approaching the speed of light it is very marked.

In the upshot the distance between two points in space has had to be replaced by what is termed the interval, which is dependent on time as well as space. Further, the proportions in which these two elements enter into a given interval depend on the speed of the observer. The interval between two points, or, in the new language, point-events, will be the same for two observers who have different speeds relative to each other; but they will each reckon time and space differently.

This result shows conclusively that space and time are forms of thought, and that they are not forms of things. Our minds produce space and time by some alchemy out of an underlying mystery called space-time, in which they are both merged. The external world, therefore, has no form which can be attributed to it. Indeed form turns out to be a mode of existence which is a fiction of our minds. What the reality behind the fiction may be is unutterably mysterious.

Once more, if reality has no form it can have no motion. We have already seen in speaking of the atom that it has no substance. On this showing what becomes of the law of Nature? The cause and effect that we observe in our daily lives must be attributes of a shadow world created by our minds. The real world which casts the shadow exists, but its mode of existence in space-time is unthinkable.

Cause and effect as we know them cannot exist in it, because cause and effect cannot exist apart from space and time and reality does not recognize space and time as independent entities.

Clearly our ideas as to the laws of Nature had to be recast

in a form which would not involve conceptions like those of force, or even permanence. They were so recast by Einstein and others after a drastic pruning which involved the abandonment of Newton's law of gravity, and the recasting of our ideas as to the conservation of mass, the conservation of energy, and allied conceptions.

The theory of relativity was expanded by the genius of Einstein to explain the motions of the planets as being the result of curvatures in space-time, caused by material masses, which are themselves higher curvatures. The explanation, of course, did not explain; but it did what was required of it, in that it enabled us to predict the motions of the heavenly bodies more accurately than the Newtonian theory.

This, then, is what the laws of Nature now amount to. They are descriptions of what happens in the form of equations generally of space-time equations, that is to say, equations involving four dimensions, of which three relate to space and one to time. The virtue of this method of stating a law of Nature is that it works out equally for the man on this planet and for his opposite number on some runaway star. I must add that, though the equations seem to correspond to special curvatures, it does not appear that it is necessary to suppose that space-time is actually curved. We cannot make any concrete suppositions about a thing of which the mind can make no picture.

We have seen that matter is a form of energy operating in a relatively vast void. Light is also a form of energy which is allied to that displayed in the atom, in that it obeys the law of gravity. In dealing with conceptions such as those which we have been discussing we must expect to find that our minds are occasionally bewildered. We may think we know that whatever radiation is it is not corpuscular.

We would be wrong. Radiation is also a corpuscular activity. Similarly, if we assume that matter cannot be radiation, whatever else it is, we would be equally wrong. It acts at times as a radiation. These contradictions are due to the fact that we are not, in dealing with ultimate things, dealing with time and space but with space-time.

Space-time is the seat of a mysterious cosmic form of energy which has received the name of action. Action is energy, as we know it, multiplied by time. Energy in this form appears to be cut up into universally equal parcels called quanta. The conception is infinitely mysterious; but it must correspond to some deep-seated truth, because it works. It explains facts that would otherwise be inexplicable.

Well, what of the man and what of his reason? The modern man of science has travelled a long way from his materialistic forbears in the last century. Modern science compels him to revise his views, not only of the universe, but of his own mental powers. Those powers are exercised on facts of two kinds. One kind embraces facts which can be made the subject of physical experiments—the facts dealt with by science—the other consists in the facts which lie outside that limited range.

They are the facts which interest the artist, the moralist, the believer in the supernatural. They are roughly included in the formula "beauty, truth and goodness". Truth in this phrase includes truth perceived as the result of intuition. The first set of facts are generally termed the commensurables and the second the incommensurables. Now modern science tells us that at bottom all truth is incommensurable. We cannot deal with the atom without employing intuitions as to its nature, as the basis of our mathematics, and these intuitions are not picturable to our reason.

As already stated the atom is a mystery and every mystery is incommensurable. Space-time is incommensurable because it includes in a mysterious merger both space and time. It fuses the forms of thought which lie at the base of all mensuration. Action is not commensurable for the same reason. It looks as if all our knowledge of real things is at bottom incommensurable. If this is the case, our intuitions of goodness, truth, and beauty may be realities of exactly the same order as space-time, action and the atom. The universe may be a mental and not a material phenomenon. To Whom does the mentality belong?

This is the question that is now being asked by the

scientists as well as by ordinary men. It is the question which ordinary men have asked and answered since history began. They have not all found the same answer; but that is a detail.

When then is the function of reason? It is built on the concepts of language and the axioms of mathematics. Both concepts and axioms are constructed out of our experience of the world of three dimensions. It cannot therefore go beyond this limitation. In other words, the truths of reason are truths which relate to the world perceived by our senses.

They do not help us to find four dimensional truth. That truth must be perceived by intuition, or else remain unperceived. The intuition may in certain cases have to be imparted in a form into which reason enters later, as when a wave theory of the atom is presented in the form of an equation. In the same way an intuition of God has to be imparted in words, and with a show of reason, which the materialistic philosopher has hitherto delighted in demolishing. We have an intuition of free will which he has demolished in the same way. None the less the materialistic philosopher shows by the fact of his argument that he disbelieves in its validity.

And, of course, no man in practice ever disbelieved in free will on any argument. It may be presumed that free will is one of the ultimates which operates in the realm of action, and may be a part of that mysterious energy.

To limit reason is not to discredit it. Its usefulness in dealing with material aggregates is as great in the twentieth as it was in the nineteenth century. It will be greater if recognition of the fundamental truth of the great intuitions of religion and morality is restored. Under this condition we may hope that human intelligence will not continue to undermine itself by efforts which are simultaneously and impartially directed to the preservation and the destruction of mankind.

If mankind comes to see that mere reason is incapable of either governing or guiding a nation, we may hope to be spared a repetition of the slaughter which, twice in a lifetime, has taken place all over the world.

Here I must draw attention to certain experimental confirmations of the conclusions of modern science. One of these relates to prophecy. Scientific men have generally disbelieved in prophecy, since Hume told them that it is one of the things that cannot take place.

Well, a Mr. Dunne noticed that certain features of his dreams came true in waking life. He got a few friends to help him, and together they made a practice of making an immediate record of their dreams. In the result a number of confirmations in waking life were obtained which are so curious and so numerous as to preclude all theories which might attribute them to chance.

Mr. Dunne wrote a book about these experiences entitled *An Experiment with Time*[1]. In it he holds that in dreams (and possibly in other states also) it is possible to survey the future as one surveys a plain from a hill. Now this is exactly the conclusion come to by the mathematician Minkowski in dealing with the primary space-time equation. He noticed that space and time enter this equation in precisely the same manner, and that, therefore, space and time must be equivalent to each other. He concluded that time is a space dimension which is imperfectly understood by our senses.

The next matter concerns experiments in clairvoyance and telepathy conducted by Professor Rhine in the United States. He found that certain subjects were able to name cards turned up by the experimenter, and, of course, unseen by them, with a degree of accuracy which precluded all idea of chance. Some of his subjects could do this at a great distance from the scene of the fall of the cards. They could name the cards even when they were dealt only in the imagination of the experimenter. The subjects were unconscious of using any sense localizable in their bodies.

The conclusion seems to be that the mind can be as independent of space as Dunne shows it to be of time. It has mysterious powers, which in the last century scientists would not have deigned to investigate.

[1] Faber & Faber.

Finally we come to the most old-fashioned manifestation of the supernatural—the miracle of healing. Miracles do occur at Lourdes. They are observed by scientists. Dr. Carrel saw one take place with his own eyes, and describes exactly what happened in his book, *Man the Unknown.*

Here we are reminded that all of these things have been known to tradition and believed in by mankind throughout the ages. Prophets, seers, and wonder workers are no new things. What is new is the dogmatic disbelief in the possibility of their existence. With facts like these before him the materialist would be hard put to it to say what is a miracle, or what event can be described as impossible.

In this connection reference may be made to an interesting description given by Dr. Carrel of the cells of the human body, and the plan on which they appear to do their work of forming and maintaining it.

He shows that the old idea that they are comparatively simple structures is entirely wrong. They are, on the contrary, exceedingly complex. Each cell has complicated organs, and a nucleus, which contains the chromosomes and genes peculiar to its inheritance. The impregnated cell from which the human being starts multiplies by a continuous process of fissure, and the cells which proceed from this operation at once begin building the body on a plan of which each cell appears to have foreknowledge. Each as it is formed goes about its work of building the organ to which it is assigned and for which it has been peculiarly fitted by the cells which preceded it. In this manner is man made.

Carrel compares the process to the building of a fairy house from a single brick which multiplies itself. The bricks thus formed make walls on a plan previously known to them; they modify themselves into doors, windows and slates; they make themselves into a sewage system; they arrange for the lighting. Not content with this they end by making, or accommodating, the owner—if we may so regard the consciousness that finally takes charge.

Now these cells have no senses which we can recognize

as such. That they have intelligence is shown by the result of their work. They appear to operate outside time, since they have absolute foreknowledge of what they have to do. We can only conclude that they furnish examples of intelligences which operate in the four dimensional continuum. That they should not only produce the human body, but provide it with a mind, which works on principles utterly foreign to their own, constitutes a recurrent miracle at which we can only gasp in wonder.

The Universe may be full of intelligences which are equally efficient and equally foreign to our own. Moreover, if those intelligences are so far apart as those of the cells from the mind of man, it follows that there must be as many universes as there are diverse intelligences. What to each of such intelligences is meant by reason? In the infinite complexity of things and beings, the human mind is indeed a poor guide, in so far as that mind depends on reason alone.

In these circumstances it would appear to be wise to investigate whether a return to belief in revelation will not produce better results.

The belief in reason—unaided reason—has been tried out. It has not succeeded. It cannot tell man the object of his existence, and therefore leaves him groping after "reasonable" ideals, which are successively tried and successively found wanting. The worshippers of will and of the superman achieve futility.

The seeker after Nirvana is in the same case. Many of us remember the Religion of Humanity and the Church which it set up in London toward the end of the last century. It achieved nothing but a futile and dreary cynicism. The worship of man by himself can hardly have any other result.

Finally, we get the worship of reason, as exemplified by the doctrines of Communism and the writings of Karl Marx. This, the last and greatest experiment in materialism, has resulted in the setting up of a great state, and in a world-wide propaganda which threatens to destroy civilization. This state has been set up on the basis of the denial of God, and of the validity of all that religion teaches. Unless the progress of Communist propaganda can be stopped it is certain that it will cost humanity vastly more suffering and vastly more slaughter.

Surely it is the duty of men of science of the twentieth century to do what they can to undo the mischief which has resulted from the teachings of their predecessors.

One suspects that, as a class, men of science are reluctant to carry their findings to the philosophical limits which they imply and necessitate. They do not wish to become philosophers. They feel the firm ground, on which their work has hitherto been based, slipping beneath their feet. They view the illimitable mysteries, which lie beyond the frontiers to which reason has led them, with alarm and misgiving. They have achieved, or at any rate received, a vision of reality, which they cannot bring themselves to proclaim.

If they hesitate they are lost. Science and all that it stands for will crash with the crash of civilization. Nothing can stop the progress of disruption except the authoritative teaching by men of scientific note and achievement that materialism is based on a false view of science.

There are indications that some of them realize this. Dr. Carrel emphatically does. Ouspensky, the Russian philosopher scientist, did. His *Tertium Organum* was published in 1924 in an excellent English translation by Alfred A. Knopf, of New York. This remarkable work has not received the attention it deserves. This book is greatly indebted to it.

After all, science should be proud of having led men to what is in effect a new revelation. It has shown definitely what the human race has always known, that reason does not and cannot, cover all the activities and all the meaning of life. All scientific knowledge must in the limit deal with the incommensurable, and can only do this by utilizing some form of intuition. Hence the ultimates of science are on precisely the same footing as our intuitions of goodness, of truth, of beauty, of God. All, so far as we know, are equally real.

[24]

The value of each can only be estimated by results. It is probable that the value so obtained represents in some mysterious way a measure of ultimate reality. The modern world has experimented in conducting the lives and government of men in accordance with the dictates of reason, as opposed to the teachings and tenets of the Christian religion.

The opposition was genuinely believed to exist. But for this belief, it is unlikely that the experiment would have been tried; since, in the long run, men's beliefs are the main influence in their lives. We cannot say that it has failed, since the Russian State continues to exist as a formidable power.

When it becomes the mark of an ill-instructed intelligence to support the doctrines of materialism their efforts will receive a decisive check. By the time that happens we may expect a revival of religion. Man must believe in something, and that something has always been a supernatural revelation, till the materialists told him that he was believing in the impossible. He will be relieved to find that the materialist was, and is, wrong.

When that takes place the world will once more become a scene of adventure. The Christian's life has a romantic quality, on which Chesterton has well insisted. If you are good you will be happy. If you fight the good fight in this life you will have achieved something of great and lasting import. You will have been faithful to a higher loyalty in a world of mysterious struggles and equally mysterious rewards. In the cosmic struggle between good and evil, which is dimly apprehended though its nature cannot be understood by us, the practising Christian feels that he is on the right side. The struggle may be hard, but it is always worthwhile. The love of God indeed passes all understanding, but it illumines the path we tread.

If modern science has shown that we are at liberty to believe in the great romance of the Christian faith, to hold that we have faculties and intuitions which correspond to realities transcending those ascertained by the use of reason, then science has given the world a revelation of inestimable value.

Men of science have, ever since the time of the great awakening of the renaissance, been distinguished for following faithfully a noble ideal—the ideal of scientific truth. They have followed it through opposition from the side of religion, which in the end ranged them against religion. They have followed it along a path lit by material triumph, but darkened by despair—despair for man's destiny—in a world which appeared to be merely the antechamber of death. They have gone on till, at the long last, we begin to see that their faith has justified not only themselves but their opponents, by enabling both to enter a realm of mysterious and splendid romance.

It is, however, a mistake to suppose that a fairly general return to religious faith will reform the world. All men are not constructed to accept easily the Christian message. In the early days of faith, when its practice was illegal and therefore perilous, Christians were no doubt men who believed and practised the tenets of the faith they professed. The change introduced by the legalization of Christianity, and still more by wholesale and forcible conversions to that faith, produced in the end a European population which professed belief *en masse.*

It is, however, doubtful whether this state of affairs has produced a very much larger proportion of real Christians than in the days of Constantine. The real heathens of to-day are mostly nominal Christians in countries in which Christianity is the prevailing faith. In a country like Russia, where it is not the prevailing faith, we are, or were, presented with a repetition of the conditions faced by the early Church, in which a courageous and believing few face a hostile and dangerous world.

It appears, therefore, that a majority of mankind are not at heart Christians; but that they are ready to profess any form of belief or disbelief which circumstances show to be necessary to their comfort or advancement. That that majority includes a number of men who are in a sort of natural opposition to religion also appears to be the fact. To quote Chesterton's remarkable words—all the more remarkable because they were penned long before the Soviet Republic was thought of:

Christianity is not so high in the air but that great archers spend their whole lives in shooting arrows at it—yes, and their last arrows; there are men who will ruin themselves and ruin their civilization if they may also ruin this old fantastic tale. This is the last and most astounding fact about this faith; that its enemies will use any weapons against it, the swords that cut their own fingers and the firebrands that burn their own homes. Men who begin to fight the Church for the sake of freedom and humanity end by flinging away freedom and humanity (orthodoxy) if only they may fight the Church.

On Christian and on scientific principles alike—I refer of course to modern scientific principles—there is nothing to indicate that there will ever be a millennium in this life on earth. On Christian principles the kingdom of heaven is not of this world. On scientific principles reality is not of this world. Therefore, if there is an ultimate reality, an ultimate reward, as the Christian religion teaches, it cannot be of this world. It is indeed curious how the evidence converges.

This world is the preparation for an ultimate reality. What that reality is like neither reason nor science can tell us. Religion tells us that it is worth striving for and most men have an intuition that religion is right.

Someone has recently said that it is curious how the scientists, who commenced by blaming philosophers because they do not follow the method of experiment, are now forced by their own experiments to become philosophers themselves.

This book is written in order to beg them to rise to the height they have reached, to become worthy of their own ideals, by carrying their scientific knowledge to its logical and philosophical conclusion. Science commenced by exploring the physical world with the aid of reason. It has ended by showing the limitations of that world, of the mind that conducts the explorations, and of reason itself.

The external world is related to the real world of four

dimensions as the shadow is related to the substance. The human mind is limited by self-created barriers of space and time, which have no counterpart outside that mind. Reason is an instrument which operates by using the concepts of language and the axioms of mathematics; but, as both concepts and axioms are built on three dimensional experience, it follows that the reason which depends on them cannot transcend it.

Science is now, I take it, assured of the existence of a four-dimensional world inhabited by such entities as action, electrons, and protons, each and all of which are fundamentally mysterious and incommensurable. In these attributes they stand on the same footing as the intuitions of religion or of the artist. All are equally entitled to be called real. All are equally inaccessible to reason. All may be entities which have a real existence in the four dimensional continuum. Indeed intuition and revelation may well be two descriptions of the same phenomenon.

Science has indeed performed wonders. If those entitled to speak in its name would only stand forth and proclaim their full meaning, and at the same time denounce the false materialism which masquerades in the name of scientific truth, they would be striking a blow for the civilization which has made their work possible.

CHAPTER II

A NEW MONADOLOGY

God and Survival

THIS and the succeeding chapter were written while I was yet expecting that the appeal to men of science contained in the first chapter would be answered. As time passed the expectation died down, and I embarked on writing the book that is now before the reader. It was and is a matter of considerable astonishment to me that a task of such obvious necessity, and one so clearly indicated by the growth of scientific knowledge, should have been left to a writer without special training in the subjects with which he deals.

In the previous chapter I have discussed the general arguments against materialism, which have resulted from the findings of modern science. I have urged that scientists ought to combine to make those findings effectively known, in order to stop the debacle of public and private morality, which has accompanied a widespread acceptance of the doctrines of materialism, and to counter the atheism which accompanies it.

In the present chapter I propose to point out a direction in which modern science has supplied a metaphysic, a description, of the universe, which admits of belief in both religion and morality. By morality I mean the morality in which all forms of the Christian religion are interested.

The proposed metaphysic is not a discovery of my own. It originated with the great Leibnitz in 1646. It is an adaptation of his philosophy of monads to the findings of modern science.

My approach to the subject is neither that of the trained scientist, nor that of the professed philosopher. It is, or tries to be, that of Christian common sense. It will therefore be realized that the standard I have set for myself is in some respects higher than that indicated by either of the other two.

There are many indications that modern physicists are feeling their way towards a transcendental form of philosophy. Eddington and Jeans, each from a somewhat different point of view, regard the universe as a mental rather than as a material phenomenon. I infer that both of them are inclined to hold that life, or lives, which possess the requisite mentality lie at the base of all things.

Professor Whitehead, too, bases his valuable philosophy of patterns on what he terms organic mechanism. I gather that he means by this, that the ultimate constituents of Nature, the electrons, protons, photons, and so on, are *purposive*, and therefore *living*, entities.

P. D. Ouspensky, the Russian philosopher scientist, is a thoroughgoing believer in the omnipresence of life in the universe; though he appears to base his belief rather on a form of intuition than on formal argument.

I think, therefore, that I have justification for claiming that I have scientific support in venturing on an interpretation of the findings of science in monadic terms.

Let us see in what Leibnitz's view consists. I quote from the article entitled *Pluralism* in the *Encyclopædia Britannica*. It is written by C. A. Richardson—a well known authority. He says:

In his famous work, the *Monadology*, he [Leibnitz] elaborated the theory that reality consists of an infinite number of individual forces or agents, psychic in nature, which he termed 'monads'.

These individual minds or spirits exhibit every degree of mental development and complexity, from that of beings even higher than men (the 'angels') right down to that of psychic entities of so low an order that Leibnitz described their being as a *mens momentanea* or a mere flash of conscious awareness. In this hierarchy of mind a complete continuity from one level of development to another was postulated

Leibnitz conceived each monad as reflecting within itself, the rest of the universe from its own particular standpoint.

This simple statement of the essentials of Leibnitz's metaphysic is sufficient for my present purpose. I do not propose to concern myself overmuch with its difficulties.

The question of the interaction of my monads will not arise in its philosophical sense, as I am here concerned with the facts, not the means, of that interaction. Nor will I enter on speculations as to how the monadic development had its beginning. I will merely indicate that on the modern view of time they have little meaning. I will, however, indicate my view (based on that of Professor Whitehead) that the monadic hierarchy ends in God, as conceived by the Christian religions.

Let us now turn our attention to the facts.

I shall assume that the ultimate reality of sensory experience lies in space-time. That continuum is of course the matrix from which our minds by some mysterious alchemy have fashioned space and time and in which neither has a separate identity.

The material objects of sense are not what our senses represent them to be. They consist of mysterious vibrations, which we call electrons, protons, and so forth. These ultimate vibrants combine to form atoms. I assume, also, that energy is a denizen of space-time exhibiting itself in the form of what is known as "action". It is a mysterious four-dimensional entity. It establishes the fact that energy cannot be infinitely subdivided. It must be communicated in integral multiples of a unit quantity called "h".

I assume finally that the ultimate vibrants are themselves denizens of space-time. I do so, although I am aware that up to the present it has not been found possible to deal with them individually by means of space-time equations.

It is a commonplace of physics that the equations hitherto employed are unsatisfactory, precisely because they fail to *locate* the vibrants in any intelligible scheme of space and time.

I need not remind my readers that in the macrocosm the Einsteinian space-time equations are the standard instruments of research.

[31]

Well, let us see whether the original vibrants can reasonably be regarded as entities which are endowed with life, and purpose, on the plan outlined by Leibnitz. I use the terms life and purpose because I wish to avoid confusion at the outset. The two terms are really synonymous.

We must begin with Heisenberg's famous principle of indeterminacy. We want to be able to predict where an electron will be a second hence. To do so we must know where it is now, and what is the state of its motion. Now the electron is a very small body—so small that it will fall within the long wave length of a feeble ray of light. It is also so light that a powerful ray of light with short wave length will disturb its motion.

It follows that with a light of long wave length we can observe its motion without much error; but that we cannot observe its position. *Per contra* with light of short wave length we may observe the position; but only at the cost of making observation of the motion meaningless. Whatever wave length between these extremes is selected there will be a definite error, and the dimensions of that error are so great as to make significant observation impossible.

Under these circumstance we cannot say what an individual electron will do. We cannot assume that it acts under some law of causation, because we cannot assume the existence of a law, which we can never observe. Professor Lindemann attributes the difficulty very neatly to the following effect.

Let us suppose that we want to know what the colour of an electron is in the dark, knowing that as soon as light is thrown upon it it will appear to be white. We are entering on an undertaking which is meaningless, because, by the nature of our premises, we can never know what the colour is. We can never observe it, and, therefore, cannot speculate about it.

Under these circumstances it is evident that no theory as to the activities of the electron can be based on observation. Recourse must be had to some method of estimating the mean behaviour of a vast number of electrons.

The celebrated wave-packet theory proceeds on this

principle. In essence, it is the same as that followed by a life insurance office. The office uses mortality tables compiled from a great number of instances, which show the probabilities of survival, for the periods required, at every age. A given individual may die sooner or later than the time indicated by the tables, but events in the former class will balance those in the latter. In the result, the predictions of the tables will, if they are carefully constructed, be substantially realized.

It is the same with the theories of the electron.

If a theory is sound, the defects from the norm, which it assumes, will be balanced by the excesses. In the result, we will have a scheme which produces reliable predictions as to the behaviour of atoms in the mass. Neither the defects, nor the excesses will be observable. As in the case of the insurance tables, the theory tells us nothing about the behaviour of any given electron. It proceeds on the assumption that the behaviour of the individual is unpredictable.

The soundness of this procedure is established, not only by its success in producing working theories, but also by an unforeseen circumstance. It was found that interior electrons could be ejected from atoms by mechanical means with an ease, which was wholly unexpected. This is now accounted for by the circumstance, foretold by the type of theory we have been considering, that a roughly predictable number of electrons will always occupy positions in which their attachment to the nucleus is weak.

In the upshot, it is evident that successful theories of the behaviour of the atom proceed on the same essential assumptions as those made by insurance companies about the deaths of human beings. They are akin to the assumptions made in interpreting all kinds of vital statistics.

In other words, the electron has to be treated as if it were a vital entity—as if it were alive.

There are other indications of the truth of this assumption. The vibrants, of which the electron is the outstanding example, combine to form atoms on plans which are often very complicated. Atomic structures increase in complexity as they

C

rise in the scale from the relatively simple atom of hydrogen. The combination of one electron with a proton might be the result of a mechanical type of causation.

But how about the more complex atoms?

To take an extreme instance, let us consider one of the radium atoms—say number eighty-eight. The complexity of this atom is enormous. Anyone who wants to assure himself of this has only to consult the model constructed after the Bohr scheme. It is reproduced in J. G. Crowther's handy *Outline of the Universe* which is printed in the Pelican series. To make it eighty-eight electrons have to combine. To do so they must get into phase, in accordance with complicated specifications which are in some fashion known to them. The enterprise must be one of considerable difficulty.

Assuming that the electrons are all very much alike, as alike shall we say as soldiers in a given military formation, how does each individual vibrant arrange with the others to take up the position that it ultimately occupies?

If we assume that the electrons are not living entities, we cannot answer the question at all. If, however, we assume that each electron is alive, and that it *wants* to make a radium atom together with a company of like-minded companions, on a plan of which each is aware, we make the only assumption that fits the facts. We assume no more in the case of the electrons than what takes place when a company of soldiers take up a military formation; but, we can assume no less.

It is no doubt wonderful that the electrons should have foreknowledge of the plan to which they conform. It is not, however, more wonderful than the behaviour of the body cells in making and maintaining the far more complicated mechanism of the body. In the case of the cells, also, the fact of prevision is equally understanding, and equally mysterious.

If the presence of life is held to explain the purposive activities of the cells, it must equally be held to explain the activities of the electrons.

It is, in either case, the only explanation that conveys an intelligible meaning.

Once more; if the vibrants are endowed with life, intelligence, purpose and foreknowledge, it is to be expected that they will find alternative means of producing a given atom within the range of the general plan. I had almost said within the meaning of the act. This is what we always find in organic units.

We find it also in the inorganic. Isotopes are of course the case in point. Some substances have more than one isotope. Tin has eleven. All substances may have isotopes, though in certain cases they may be too rare to detect.

Finally, to complete the resemblance of the conduct of the vibrants to that of living cells, we note that in the case of certain complicated atoms—those in the radio-active category —the task of maintaining the atom in existence appears to be onerous.

In the case of the radium atom, we can only suppose that the vibrants have never quite succeeded in getting into phase, and that, in consequence, the subsequent maintenance of the atom in being involves a constant state of strain. As we know, the strain tells in the end, and the atom explodes. This reason for the explosion of radium atoms is in full accord with the fact that no way has been found of predicting the explosions.

It is, of course, possible that the radio-active elements are not the only elements, which experience explosions. In stable atoms, if they ever take place, they can do so only rarely, so rarely, indeed that observation of their occurrence is virtually impossible.

Let us now turn to the society of vibrants that we call the atom.

Here we have another unit, that acts as if it were alive. Atoms combine to form crystals, and molecules.

In both cases they take up formations, which are often very complicated, and of which they appear to have complete foreknowledge. In making these formations they act precisely like the vibrants, that is to say, as if they were living units, endowed with intelligence, foreknowledge, and purpose. We can only compare their behaviour with that of cells, or soldiers. We cannot account for it on any mechanistic scheme.

The continuation of the argument is sufficiently obvious. The unit crystals and molecules act as if they were fresh personalities. The former form themselves into ranks, which interlock in ways that are generally complicated. The latter enter into all the chemical combinations with which the chemist deals, from such simple substances as water to the most complicated carbon compounds.

Without dwelling further on the vital aspects displayed by the chemical compounds as they become successively more complicated, we must note, in passing, that on our planet life, in the forms in which it is generally recognized—the so-called organic forms—is associated exclusively with the carbon compounds. The colloids, and the viruses have been held to lie on the boundary, which marks off the organic from the inorganic.

On the showing of this book, of course, no such boundary exists. Every natural unit is a living personality, which in all cases, except that of the basic vibrants, is constituted from other personalities.

It will, none the less, be convenient to continue to speak of the organic and the inorganic sides of Nature in order to avoid circumlocution.

As soon as organic life appears we have a new set of conditions. This form of life is distinguished from the inorganic form, *inter alia*, by the facts that the units embark on processes such as nutrition, and reproduction. Another discrimination is provided by the presence of an enormous mass of observable variations.

It is probably true to say that no two organisms of the same species are quite alike. We are not sure that any two inorganic compounds are precisely similar, and it is quite possible that they are not. It would seem, however, that such variations as may exist in the inorganic entities are, in general, too minute to be observed with our instruments.[1] A

[1] At this point the reader is referred to the discussion of the phenomena produced by particle bombardment on page 102 of Chapter VI.

peculiar feature of the greater living organisms is that they are built up from cells, which are themselves complicated life units.

For our present purpose we will dwell on one only of these features. The existence of a mass of variations is inconsistent with any theory which regards life as having been *mechanically* produced from dead material. Such a theory always assumes that inorganic compounds are precisely similar to one another, when their chemical constituents are the same. But homogeneous antecedents cannot be expected to give rise to the phenomenon of variation.

If it be conceded that the inorganic antecedents may be themselves dissimilar, we find ourselves embarked on a series of concessions to the vital theory, which ends by requiring us to assume that the vibrants differ from each other. This is almost certainly the case; but the concession is fatal to the mechanistic point of view. On the vital theory, variations may have come into existence from the purposive efforts of each organism to adapt itself to its environment, and it may be that they tend to be inherited because they proceed from within, and are not impressed on the organism by its environment.

The dogma which states that acquired characteristics are not heritable, can only refer to characteristics which are imposed on the organism from outside. Variations arising from the spontaneous efforts of the organism itself may well modify the genes, and so become heritable. It thus appears that the theory set forth in this book provides an explanation of the profusion of variation in organic nature.

It is foreign to my purpose to pursue the development of organic forms from the cell to man. There are various theories on the subject, most, if not all, of which are tentative, and all of which are unsatisfactory.

It suffices to say that, throughout both inorganic and organic nature, we have an ascending series of personalities, which interlock with each other in an ascending scale of complexity.

We must now turn to a matter of very great interest and significance.

If life and personality begin with the vibrants, they must exist throughout the universe.[1] The sun and the stars, no less than the earth, must be constituted from them. In the sun and the stars they may show developments of personality based on increasing complexity, precisely as on the earth; but these developments will not be dependent on the presence of carbon compounds.

Such personalities would be capable of existing in all ranges of temperature, and under all conditions of pressure, and of its absence. We, of course, have no knowledge of their existence. Like the cells, they may have no organs that we could recognize. As in the case of the cells, again, the universe will be to them something wholly different from what it appears to us.

A dimension of space may to them be a dimension of time. They may be exceedingly active, and intelligent entities, but busied about matters of which we can form no picture and can have no comprehension.

On the general theory of space-time something of this sort is to be expected. If our world is a projection of the space-time world of reality, then there may be a vast number of such projections, each peculiar to its appropriate types of personalities, and each a development along a separate line of chemical combination.

The forms taken by what we call reason in these alien personalities must be wholly beyond our comprehension. We might infer the presence of reason from the result of their activities, when such could be distinguished, and in the case of the body cells we *must* make this inference. Further than this we can hardly go.

If, however, the alien personalities deal with their several universes in a manner analogous to that in which we deal with ours, it would be open to all of them to infer the existence of a world of reality transcending their shadow worlds; and,

[1] It is here relevant to note that no atom is inert even when external excitation is absent. It is always accepting or giving out energy. This has been established by the great Einstein as the result of a celebrated research. The phenomenon is consistent with our vital theory, though difficult to reconcile with views which regard atoms as inanimate, and therefore "dead" entities.

for each of them, that world of reality would be the same world. In other words, there would be one space-time for all personalities, wherever situated, and however alien they might be from each other.

One of the most difficult problems for the Christian, and for everyone who wishes to believe in the divine guidance of the universe, is precisely the apparent waste which takes place in confining personality and intelligence to one or possibly to two or three planets.

On the scheme here explained it is unnecessary to assume that such waste exists. On that scheme we are at liberty to hold that the universe is a vast concourse of personalities, each after its manner working out the purpose of the Almighty, against a common background of reality.

The monads of Leibnitz were assumed by him to be windowless. That is to say, they could not communicate with each other. Each was regarded as a closed system. This is not the case with the monads with which modern science has provided us. In their case we must assume that monads of the same kind can communicate with one another, since nothing else will explain the fact that they are able to combine. Monads, which are greatly unlike one another, which belong to different orders in the chain of being, may of course be unable to communicate with each other.

A difficulty inherent in a monadology is that it seems impossible to account for the beginning of the system. We deal with a scheme of development, which can be traced to no origin. Well, I do not think that this difficulty arises on a proper appreciation of the nature of space-time.

In space-time time is one with space. That is to say, it has no beginning. What we regard as the necessity for all things to have a beginning is due to the structure of our minds. We cannot realize that the notion of a beginning is bound up with the notion of a time which is fundamentally distinct from space. Such a time does not exist. It appears to exist in the three-dimensional continuum; but that continuum is itself unreal.

A personality which suddenly found itself free from all

the associations of the body, and all its functions, would experience a continuum in which it would be conscious of itself and of its value in the great scheme of things. It would not be conscious of any passage of three-dimensional time. There would be no beginning to which it could look back, and no ending to which it could look forward. The question of a four-dimensional time does not arise here. It will be dealt with in later chapters.

These considerations are inherent in the nature of space-time, since, in that continuum, time becomes a fully revealed, instead of as now an imperfectly understood, dimension of space. We cannot understand such conditions with the logical mind; but to the perceptions of intuition, or, shall we say, through revelation, they are not only acceptable, but natural.

The notion that in the afterlife time shall be no more, which is found in the Scriptures, is just such a revelation, and one from which the mind cannot be said to revolt. The space-time continuum is a continuum in which both form and movement are non-existent, being replaced by energies and activities, of which the human mind can form no picture. The scientist is as much bound to assume the existence of this "real" continuum as the Christian is to believe in the existence of the Kingdom of Heaven. They may be one and the same thing. They almost certainly are.

Of course, the whole conception of living wholly, instead of, as now, partially, in the realm of reality bristles with mental difficulties. We can form no logical picture of it. But then we can form no logical idea of what constitutes the entities, which, as we have seen, must be regarded as the aboriginal denizens of space-time. I refer of course to entities such as light, which is conceived of as "travelling" through a continuum, which is nothing but the background of a space-time equation.

We cannot conceive of the nature of "action", though we know that it represents the reality behind what we call energy. We cannot conceive of the existence of the vibrants, of which it has to be said that there is nothing which vibrates; that the completed vibration *is* the entity.

It might be considered that the views expressed in this chapter are new and fanciful. This is not the case.

We have seen already that the philosophy of monads, that is to say the philosophy we have been discussing, goes back to the great Leibnitz, a distance in time of nearly three hundred years. What is new is a scientific outlook, which supports, and (in my view) necessitates, a belief in that philosophy. The notion of a real world, that is to say of the continuum which is now called space-time, is vastly older. It arose both among the ancient Greeks and among the Hindus. The ancient Greek philosopher Parmenides held views which are startlingly modern on the subject. I find the following account of them in the *Encyclopædia Britannica*:

. . . . he regarded reality as eternal, uncreated, and imperishable. There is no empty space, "all is full of being", and so there is no possibility of motion. Reality was apparently a finite, spherical, motionless, continuous plenum, and change, movement, and the very existence of ordinary discrete things illusory.

Translating into modern terms, so as to make it clear that empty space must be replaced by the motion of a curved space-time; that motion, being a function of time and space, is unthinkable in the space-time continuum; that change is unthinkable for the same reason; that form, being a function of the space of sensory experience, is equally illusory; and, finally, that, on the above showing, the existence of "ordinary, discrete things" is an illusion; we reach an interpretation of Parmenides which might almost be an interpretation of the views of Sir James Jeans in his mysterious universe. Parmenides' view that "all is full of being" is again most interesting. It makes him a forerunner of Leibnitz and a near-contemporary of the Hindu mystic philosophers.

Plato is, of course, the originator of many conceptions which are only now coming into their own. Readers of *The Mysterious Universe* will remember the translation of his parable of the shadows of the cave, which prefaces that work. It is a fanciful, but extremely accurate, description of the world of sense as a shadow, or projection, of the world of reality.

His doctrine of ideas is summed up by the author of the history of philosophy article in the *Encyclopædia Britannica* as follows. He held that "the objects of real knowledge are not the ever-changing things of the sensible world, but supra-sensible objects which are immutable and eternal." Quite; reality exists, and exists only in space-time. The learned author of *The Human Situation* (Professor Macneile Dixon) could no doubt produce fifty instances of equal appositeness from the Greek classics.

But, the Greeks were not the only people who had attained to a true notion of the nature of reality. The same intuition is the main position taken by Hindu philosophy. The sensory world is the world of illusion—of *maya*. The yogi can make no higher use of his life than to devote it to the strenuous preparations which would enable him to inhibit the functions of his body, and thus set free his soul, his personality, to enter the continuum of reality.

These penetrating glimpses into the nature of being and reality must be classed as intuitions. A better name would probably be revelation. Both terms may be identical. The wonderful thing about the present age of knowledge is that science is establishing the necessity for recognizing that the ancient intuitions, of which we have been speaking, are also scientific statements.

Those who require proof that intuition is likely to be a safe guide in the major difficulties and problems of life have it here. It is indeed the only guide when we come to deal with phenomena which are on the border-line of human perception. In that domain it presents us with physical truths in a dress of logical contradictions—a circumstance which emphasizes the mystery in which ultimate truth is shrouded from our eyes.

It is of interest to compare the modern attitude, that attitude which is at once ancient and modern, with that of the materialist. The latter is a reversion to type, to a very primitive type. Primitive peoples have always tended to worship images. "The heathen in his blindness bows down to wood and stone." The materialist rejects the image, but worships its components. The mentality in each case is precisely the same.

Of the two the heathen has a slight advantage, since he is generally broad-minded enough to recognize that a deity, which has not served his purpose, may be exchanged for another. The materialist, however, still supports "an outworn creed" as obstinately as the fundamentalist at whom he delights to jeer.

Perhaps the most important feature of modern thought is the manner in which it supports the ancient belief in God.

To indicate what I mean I will quote a celebrated passage from Professor A. N. Whitehead's book entitled, *Religion in the Making*. Here is the passage:

It is not the case that there is an actual world which accidentally happens to exhibit an order of Nature. There is an actual world because there is an order of Nature. If there were no order there would be no world. Also, since there is a world, we know that there is an order. The ordering entity is a necessary element in the metaphysical situation presented by the actual world.

. . . The metaphysical doctrine, here expounded, finds the foundation of the world in the æsthetic experience, rather than with Kant in the cognitive and conceptive experience. All order is therefore æsthetic order, and the moral order is merely certain aspects of æsthetic order. The actual world is the outcome of the æsthetic order, and the æsthetic order is derived from the immanence of God.

It will be seen that this proof of the existence of God can be illustrated from the monadic process which has been here outlined. The vibrants, atoms, molecules and so forth combine to form new compounds directed by new personalities from a directive urge, which lays down for them the plan or plans on which successful combination can be effected. Here we have the order which exhibits itself in the world, and which preceded the world.

It is a living order because it proceeds from the various

personalities or purposes which produced it under the direction of the Supreme Purpose. All effort has an æsthetic element. This follows from the fact that it can be directed well or ill; the entity which is concerned being aware of the quality of its action. It knows whether, according to its standard, it is doing or failing to do all that it can do to achieve its purpose.

We have indicated our views that the vibrants, atoms, and so forth, experience a greater or less difficulty in making the personalities and combinations which they do make; and that after they have been made they experience a greater or less difficulty in keeping them in existence. What we do not know is the extent to which these efforts have failed. We do not know how often attempts to make (say) an atom are frustrated by the conduct of one or more of the constituent vibrants. We may take it that this information will never be available to us.

We can, however, see dimly that some of the more unstable chemical compounds may, to some extent, represent failures—failures which are only partial, perhaps, but still failures to achieve what *we* must consider to be an end of the process of making personalities; namely the endurance of these personalities in the three-dimensional continuum.

Thus the order striven for even by the inorganic has æsthetic quality. The choice, which is presented to every entity on every occasion of conscious activity of being able to carry out that activity well or ill is essentially æsthetic. The alternative before the unit is not a choice of activities; it is a choice between exercising a given activity as it should be exercised, and failing to do so. From this point of view all conscious effort has an æsthetic quality. As Whitehead puts it, it follows that "The actual world is the outcome of the æsthetic order, and the æsthetic order is derived from the immanence of God."

At this point we must lay emphasis on certain aspects under which life may be viewed. Will, purpose, personality, quality, value, consciousness are all words which are applicable to life. They may indeed be taken as synonyms for the one word, life. If anything corresponding to any one of them survives, then the surviving entity has each and all of the attributes indicated by the remaining terms.

In common speech, of course, quality and value are used in relation to material objects; but this use is one which is to be excluded from my argument. I assume that quality and value are to be considered only in relation to life, whether that life be the life of a vibrant, an atom, a cell, or a man.

Further, though we do not know what any of these terms may mean as applied to entities other than man, we assume that they mean something analogous to the human meaning. Hence, when we speak of the survival of an entity, we mean that something, which may be indifferently described as will, purpose, personality, value, or consciousness survives the break-up of the organism, to which in this life it is attached.

Whitehead considers that the distinction which we make between space and time is fundamental. In other words he does not accept Einstein's space-time continuum. He has devised a mathematical formula which supports this view. It is not accepted by his brother physicists, and it is not accepted here. His contention appears to result in the view that the real world is the world in which we are conscious of living. He contemplates the evolution of that world through unending complexities to an end in which infinite complexity is the final goal. It is difficult to reconcile such a view with survival.

In my opinion, for what it is worth, Whitehead's philosophy is in its broad lines in harmony with Einstein's theory. I also think that a great deal of the difficulty that attends the reading of his work springs from the discussions necessitated by his scientifically unorthodox view of the nature of space and time. I propose to deal further with this matter in a later chapter.

Accordingly, I assume that, following Einstein and Minkowski, the reality of our sensory experience lies in the space-time continuum. In that continuum space and time are merged in something more fundamental, and have no separate existence. In that continuum there is no such thing as form. What we see as form is a shadow, a projection cast on our world of three dimensions by an activity of which we can have no sense perception; that is to say, it is something which we cannot picture.

Incidentally, the same difficulty attaches to the reality of what in our world we call motions. The most intelligible supposition to our intelligence is that in the space-time continuum time becomes a dimension akin to space. In this world therefore it may be viewed as an ill-understood space dimension. I have already referred to this.

In such a continuum the only existences which we can postulate are lives, in other words, forms of life as understood in one or all of its synonyms such as will, consciousness, intelligence, etc. On this showing life is the only real existence. Hence when we talk of survival we must mean the survival of a conscious value, a personality.

For the believer in survival death then means the introduction of the spirit (another synonym for life) to a continuum in which it becomes conscious of itself as the sum of the values which it has acquired in life. Death is in other words the introduction of the spirit to an integration of those values. The spirit knows itself for what it has made itself. As time passes, while space does not, the spirit for which time has become a dimension of space is immortal. For it time is literally no more.

It thus appears that modern science is not opposed to belief in survival, understood as we have stated it. On the contrary, that belief is consistent with its conclusions. It has already been pointed out that the forms of things cannot have any counterpart in space-time, and that the reality behind the forms is the only part of them that can survive their break-up.

A belief so based is one that satisfies human instinct. It assures man that his efforts to invest his life on earth with a value, over and above that acquired for the purpose of prolonging his earthly existence, are not wasted. His life is not a comedy or a tragedy of error. It is a preparation for something greater than this life can show, and that something is in accordance with his deepest instincts.

There is no reason to assume that with the break-up of the body the personality is destroyed, except the difficulty of realizing the essential unreality of the world of forms. That world is for us the real world, in the sense that it is the world that must be faced and defeated, if the struggle for existence is to succeed. That is why sensory experience occupies the unique position that it does in our scheme of things. That is why it is regarded as reality in a sense that is not accorded to mental experience. Modern science has done an infinite service to mankind in showing us that it is not an ultimate reality, and that there is both room and reason to look forward to a live in which values replace forms.

Students of the supernatural in its various forms such as Yogism, theosophy, spiritualism, and so forth will notice that, as a rule, the phenomena with which they deal are accompanied by (1) a certain inhibition of the senses, and (2) by descriptions of experience in the other world, which are either devoid of form or else use words involving form with the express warning that they have only a cloudy relation to the facts of that experience.

Under (1) we have a wide range of facts which tend to show that the personality can and does operate independently of the body. The trance of the Hindu Yogi may reach to the inhibition of the action of the heart and lungs, and may last for periods of something like forty days. The personality is not, however, submerged with the inhibition of the body. Far from it: the consciousness is enormously heightened. The emotions and the intellectual faculties achieve higher powers. The personality thus attains its highest power when the powers of the body are at their lowest ebb. This indicates that after death we may expect the permanent inhibition of the bodily functions to produce a similar result. In other words we may expect survival.

As to (2) it need only be said that it is in full accord with the expectation demanded by science. In the case of most mystics and specially in that of the Yogi the change in the time sense which accompanies the mystic experience is nearly always insisted on.

It is not always realized that there is a converse to the experiences we have indicated. The body may, and often does, submerge the personality. This is a common result of the bad habits or complexes, which so often overpower, and for the time being blot out, the real personality. This indicates that man can kill, or at any rate indefinitely degrade his personality, his spirit.

Here again we find emphasis laid on the independence of the two factors. In this case, however, the spirit, not the body, is the subject of the inhibition. It is probable that the only true examples of behaviourism are to be found in these phenomena of degradation. The same phenomena may furnish the interpretation of instances of double personality, of which we sometimes hear.

Yogism brings out the difference between the ideals of the Christian religion and those of the more intellectual forms of Hinduism. The Christian does not seek the mystic experience, though on rare occasions Christians obtain it. This is because the Christian is taught to utilize this life as an opportunity for creating value in the next. He does this by living for others rather than for himself.

The Hindu, on the contrary, recognizes no such obligation, and when he reaches the higher grades of his religion, concerns himself with trying to anticipate the experience of death. He does so on the ground that all earthly experience is a valueless illusion. He does not try to add to the value of his experience on earth, but rather to evade all opportunity of doing so. I speak, of course, in these general terms with the knowledge that they relate in full only to exceptional Christians and exceptional Hindus.

In conclusion I would like to quote a passage from the twenty-first chapter of Dr. Macneile Dixon's book entitled *The Human Situation*. I have taken it almost at random from a summing up which depicts the loss to humanity which a denial of survival involves. The whole chapter is a most telling piece of literature. The passage runs as follows:

If any life beyond the present be denied you need go no further. The world condemns itself. For if indeed existence offers any values it can only be to the individual human beings who have a share in existence. If there be any good and if there be any beauty it is in them and their perceptions of such things. Where else could it be? The rest is but mud and motion. And since, if the valuators perish all values, truth, goodness and the rest, go with them into everlasting night, no theological or metaphysical twittering can rebut the demonstrable hollowness of life, its inherent futility. The passing show may have its interest, but how slight and ephemeral, how painful an interest. We are offered it seems a sip from the cup of life, which is then forever withdrawn. No very munificent gift from the exalted and Almighty Absolute.

CHAPTER III

SPACE-TIME

A Link Between Religion and Science

I WISH to guard against readers being misled into thinking
that the vital theory set forth in the last chapter is more
original than it is. As a matter of fact there is very little in
it that is not either implicit or explicit in good scientific, or
philosophic, opinion. It is based, primarily, on a theory of
the universe, which originated with the great Leibnitz. It
has reappeared, partially, in the guise of "Organic Mechanism"
in Professor Whitehead's *Science and the Modern World*. What
I have called personalities, or lives, are, I believe, very much
the same as Professor Whitehead's organic mechanisms.

The theory of space-time, as we all know, originated with
Minkowski, and flowered exceedingly in the hands of his
great successor Einstein.

In the hands of another Russian, P. D. Ouspensky, the
connection between space-time and the mystic continuum
was emphasized. He lays stress on the limitations of the
human intellect, which follows alike from the mystical and the
mathematical implications of space-time. I may here refer the
reader to his *Tertium Organum*, and his *New Model of the Universe*.

I have used the materials mentioned to support a line of
argument which, considered as a whole, may have some
originality. When I came to consider the various implications
of space-time on man's outlook on the universe, I was
astounded by the practical importance of a conception,
which is still little understood by the general reading public.

A general description of space-time is given in my first
chapter, and should here be referred to. It is not a continuum
which is separate from our space and time. It includes and
envelops them. You and I live in space-time, even more

really than we live in space and time. It is, perhaps, easier to imagine it as a state than as a continuum. There are facts of life which cannot be weighed or measured, and with which, in consequence, science cannot deal. Life is such a fact.

In the last chapter, entitled *A Living Universe*, I gave reasons for holding it to be the ultimate fact—the ultimate reality— of the universe. In the same chapter I showed that the ultimate particles, which I called the vibrants—the electrons, protons and photons, can never be individually observed. They cannot, therefore, be weighed or measured. They fall in the same category as life in the fact of their being incommensurable, and modern theories of atomic structure proceed on this basis.

Again, light and all the other kinds of radiation are something over and above what our senses can perceive of them. Light is both a radiation and a corpuscular entity. It travels in a medium which has no physical existence save in the mathematical assumption which is necessitated by a space-time equation. Whatever it is that lies behind the radiatory or corpuscular phenomena is a mystery, and every mystery is incommensurable.

Energy, again, is equally mysterious. What we call energy is a product of a four dimensional activity, "action", and from this activity both matter and energy, as they appear in our world, are derived. In short, everything, when traced back to its ultimate beginning, turns out to be either incommensurable in itself, or else based on an incommensurable. In the upshot, as we have seen, this indicates that every entity, every natural entity, is a purposive life in the space-time continuum or state. That state is the state in which everything has a real existence.

Existence in space and time is a derivative of that existence. The forms and movements of the space and time continuum are, as it were, the projections of formless entities and activities, which inhibit space-time.

When a solid is sliced open it reveals a surface. In the same way, if a four dimensional solid is sliced open, a three dimensional continuum should be revealed. In other words, a universe analogous to our own of three dimensions would come into being. This means that space-time is something of which every section yields a three dimensional universe. One of these universes is our own.

It was indicated in the last chapter that there must be a large number of universes existing together in the section of space-time that constitutes our universe; since for each separate set of senses, there must be a different outlook on the world. The cell must see a different universe from that seen by the organism of which it is a component part. If the basic lives—the electrons, protons, etc.—are, as we have held, alive, it is reasonable to suppose that they have developed modes of existence in the stars, and inter-stellar spaces, which are, and which contain, composite organisms. Each such organism would see a different universe.

In the upshot, space-time is the abode of the reality behind every three dimensional universe and, since that reality consists in living entities, it must be the abode of these entities. Human beings are simultaneously inhabitants of the world of space and time, and of the continuum, or state of space-time. If we imagine ourselves as living both on and in a slice of space-time, these conditions will be fulfilled.

The incommensurable side of us comes from within the slice, and the commensurable from its surface. Our personalities, and their attributes or qualities, in the sense of values, belong to the former category, and the world of motion and form, which our senses perceive, to the latter. The motions and forms are related to the lives which constitute their "real" nature as the shadow is related to the substance, or as the plane section is related to the solid.

On the one side they are three dimensional, and on the other four dimensional. In this connection it should be remembered that in nature there cannot be a surface without depth. Every surface which is not a purely mental concept has some thickness. In the same way every three dimensional universe has a four dimensional aspect. It must exist, to some extent, in space-time. It must partake of space-time.

Both worlds are real; but each has a reality of a different kind, and the two are interwoven.

We have seen that the ultimate constituents of the universe are lives, and that these lives must be regarded as personalities. The unit personalities are the electrons, protons, and photons. From these units are built up others which are complex containing personalities. The latter in turn build up more personalities in a process which, for us, appears to end in man. All organic lives contain these personalities.

The Hindu philosophy speaks of the spirits of the body, and by this it means that the human body contains a mass of personalities subordinate to the personality which we recognize as a man. In this view it has anticipated the general theory of this book.

If these factors are to replace matter, or whatever ultimate entity the modern materialist relies on to replace it, then they must inherit the attributes of that entity. The most prominent of these attributes is immortality. Something must survive change in order that change may have a basis. If atoms are the basis of the universe, then atoms are immortal. If electrons are the basis, then electrons are immortal. If life is the basis, then lives are immortal. At any rate the unit lives must have this attribute.

Does the same presumption apply to the lives that are built up from those units? Are molecular personalities immortal? Are the personalities which are the cells immortal? Are the personalities which are organisms immortal? Is man himself immortal?

On the evidence of the mystic experience, they are. That evidence depends on human experience of a condition which is generally brought about by the inhibition of the bodily functions in various ways, more especially by the Hindu form of the mystic trance; and on the accounts given by a few persons who have been brought back from the threshold of death.

This evidence shows—to put the matter in its briefest form—that the more complete the inhibition of the bodily functions the more active become the mental and emotional powers of the person concerned. On this showing, death could seem to operate as a release of the personality concerned from the fetters of the body. More accurately, it may be regarded, in respect of the dominant personality, as a release from the restraints of the subordinate personalities with which it has in life been associated, and by which it has been limited.

This is good mystic philosophy, and may well be good science. Further, if the change that we call death is what we perceive it to be, a break-up of a physical association of physical forms, we have no reason, and logically no right, to hold that it is anything more. The realities behind the forms are lives co-ordinated by a dominating life. All of them are space-time entities, and in space-time physical change is unintelligible.

What we see in this world are the shadows cast by those entities on three dimensions. The fact that at death the shadows disappear does not necessarily mean that the reality behind the shadows is extinguished. If life is the original substance of everything, then any theory which assumes its extinction is of the nature of an assumption that neither energy, nor any other conceivable ultimate, is conserved. The assumption reduces everything to chaos.

These considerations are of course logical. They fall short, therefore, of demonstration of the thesis of survival. That is to be expected; since three dimensional reason cannot be applied satisfactorily to the four dimensional continuum in which the reality behind sensory experience has its being. The really convincing proof of survival lies in the evidence of which I have spoken—namely, the evidence of the mystics and of the revenants from death.

On this view science has done religion—all the higher religions—a great service, by helping to establish the existence of a state, in the shape of space-time, in which survival can take place. It has probably done more, since it would appear to have established the existence of a state in which survival must take place. It has, also, indicated the form which survival must take. It must be the survival of personalities invested with the qualities, the values, which they have acquired in the three dimensional existence.

Finally, it invests survival with the quality of being a continuation of the life of three dimensions. All this is wholly in accord with the religious outlook.

According to science, space-time is the seat of tremendous energies. The atom is a compact of such energy. Radiation is such an energy. We must now ask what, in the space-time state, underlies the physical and chemical phenomena which, for us, exhibit energy. In that state it takes the four dimensional form of "action". In space-time what we know as energy is multiplied by time. In this form it is not infinitely divisible. It can only be communicated in parcels, each of which is an integral multiple of a small quantity called "h".

Action is that which gives rise alike to radiation, and the ultimate vibrants. In the latter guise, as we have seen in the last chapter, it is alive, since every electron, positron, and proton is alive. We must assume that in its free form it is equally alive. It would seem that each photon, each parcel, of energy which operates on its surroundings, is a personality like the electron.

On this assumption, what we see as motion and interaction must in their real aspect be the operation of personalities on other personalities. Motion in three dimensions is, like the rest of causation, merely an exhibition of unchanging sequences. A stone falls to the ground whenever it is released from support. Hence the law of gravity. The law is, of course, nothing but the statement of the existence of an invariable sequence.

Every natural law, in the sense used by the scientists of the last century, is such a statement. It summarizes our experience, and in this aspect is enormously useful; but it does not add to our knowledge of the nature of cause and effect. The true causes lie in space-time, and in space-time they consist in the interaction of personalities. We have already seen that every natural entity is in its four dimensional essence a personality, or a complex of personalities, forming linked societies each governed by a dominating personality.

Modern science has given up the search for natural laws of the old-fashioned kind. Such laws exist as a practical convenience for those who deal with matter in its gross form. In that form matter obeys them. In its ultimate form—i.e. in the form of the ultimate vibrants—natural laws are merely statistical truths. They are not obeyed by the individual vibrants. They represent nothing more than the average conduct of those vibrants.

At the base of things there is no ascertainable uniformity. The electrons are not uniform. If they were they could not range themselves into the societies that we call atoms. They would all be trying to take the same place at the same time in the atomic societies, and atoms would never come into existence.

The atoms and molecules, being based on the vibrants, are still less uniform; since they are made up of a number of dissimilar elements. The chemical side of science consists in the tracing of an ever increasing number of combinations of ever increasing complexity through the inorganic up to, and through the (so-called) organic.

At each stage, we must suppose that there is an increase of variation. At any rate, when we come to life in its acknowledged forms, we find that variation is one of its most dominant characteristics. This is clearly due to the fact that all living organisms are an integration of a vast number of subordinate elements, each of which exhibits variation. In the chemical elements the variations exist but are not generally traceable; unless they take such obvious forms as are presented by the isotopes. But, when they are integrated over a relatively vast field, such as that presented by an animal, or an insect, they at once become apparent.

At this stage they are more than apparent. They are dominant. In this connection it may be noted that a company of soldiers engaged in forming fours, or other military formation, must be considered to be similar to each other for that purpose—similar, that is, in their readiness to carry out orders with the requisite intelligence. But it is evident that outside this function they can and do differ enormously from each other. Such differences would not necessarily come under the notice of their commanding officer.

It is the same with the electrons and the various inorganic and organic societies which are based on them. The chemist, like the commanding officer, has his attention focused on similarities, and assumes an identity between the entities with which he deals that is wholly misleading. In some cases of marked, but rare, deviation from the norm of the species under consideration, we are presented with what amounts to natural miracles.

The supernatural becomes the natural. Miracles must occur. Some electrons in each atomic society must take up positions which are (statistically considered) "impossible". All the societies derived from the atoms from the molecule to the living cell must, similarly, on occasion, exhibit variations which are "impossible". *A fortiori* animals and plants must, now and then, exhibit "impossible" variations from the standard type. In the human species, Homer, Plato, Julius Cæsar, Newton, Leibnitz, Napoleon, Einstein, are all miracles in this sense. It is, of course, the same with the lives of the founders of the great religions. It is the same with all the *true* accounts of happenings which are so strange as to deserve the name of miraculous.

In this connection we may note that various human beings possess powers which would, in the last century, have been refused the honour of investigation by a certain (and still prevalent) type of scientist on the ground of inherent incredibility.

I refer to phenomena of television and clairvoyance like those with which Professor Hine has recently concerned himself; to the instances of precognition, such as those with which the name of Dunne is prominently associated; to miraculous healings, about which the evidence is massive. These powers, and the phenomena that they produce, are in the miraculous class.

Finally, when we consider that causation in its real aspect is not the action of matter on matter (we no longer know what matter is), but of personality on personality in the continuum of space-time, there is no reason for supposing, either that miracles can never occur, or that they may not occur in greater or less abundance at different times and places. Whether an alleged miracle has or has not occurred, then becomes a question of evidence. On that evidence it is open to those who examine it to decide, each for himself, whether it has taken place or not. What is no longer open is to say that it is inherently impossible.

When it is generally recognized that certain individuals have unusual powers, a way will have been opened for their practical utilization. Dr. Carrel has stressed the desirability of viewing human beings, and specially human patients, as dominated far more by their personalities than has hitherto been customary in the medical profession. A feat of fasting which was possible for Mr. Gandhi may be impossible for most other men.

If, as we have seen, a physical law is at bottom nothing but a statistical statement, then a miracle is simply the occurrence of some extremely unlikely variation from the norm on which the law is based. The degree of improbability which would entitle a given occurrence to rank as a miracle would vary from observer to observer.

The true causes, which lie in the interaction of four dimensional personalities, are never apparent. They can never be dealt with by our reasoning apparatus. They can be perceived only by intuition. They have often been so perceived by the mystics. To an organism like a snail or a fly, which is low in the scale of being, the movement of a gigantic body, such as that of a dog at the call of his master, is assuredly a miracle.

Here we have the basic case of personality acting on personality. What is maintained in this book is that this is precisely what happens in all the manifold changes that take place in our universe. Phenomena which we recognize as due to the operation of personality on personality in our daily intercourse with men and animals are merely samples of a universal process. The importance of this view for religion is obvious.

The real world of space-time has been compared to a state. By this distinction I mean to indicate that it has none of the attributes of the space with which we are familiar. A continuum, that has nothing in it that can be likened to form, cannot resemble our space.

Hence, though Minkowski tells us that time is a space dimension which we imperfectly understand, the result of the fusion of time with space is to destroy all resemblance of the product to either space or time. This at once becomes evident when we consider that, as lines cannot be drawn or imagined in a four dimensional continuum, no axes can be set up in it whereby any mathematical properties it possesses can be dealt with.

Further, arithmetic has no meaning in space-time, since in a formless continuum nothing is discreet. Everything is at one and the same time, the one and the all. This is precisely what the mystic experience tells us about the state to which that experience relates. Number is in its nature discrete. It derives from the operation of counting, and objects which can be counted are necessarily discrete.

The mystic sometimes tells us that, in his continuum, everything is here and now. A little thought will show that this weird characteristic necessarily implies a formless continuum, and every four dimensional continuum is formless, as a matter of mathematical necessity.

If no space can be distinguished everything must be "here". If no time is perceivable everything is similarly "now".

These Alice-in-Wonderland attributes of space-time merely indicate that our reason cannot deal with a four dimensional continuum. It is based on the three dimensional experience of this world, and cannot go beyond it. The concepts of language and the axioms of mathematics alike are drawn from that experience. But it must not be concluded that because it is difficult to endow space-time with attributes that convey a meaning to our three dimensional intellects, therefore space-time is a conception which cannot concern us.

The fact is quite otherwise. We have seen that it contains the whole of the reality which lies behind three dimensional phenomena, and that our three dimensional world of form bears to it somewhat the relation that a plane section of a solid bears to that solid.

By this (as we have noted) we mean that, if space-time could be sliced open, it would reveal a three dimensional universe at each section. Hence, so far from space-time being less real than the three dimensional universe, it is infinitely more real. It contains the whole of the reality of which our three dimensional universe represents no more than a section.

On this showing a description of the Deity as being One in Three and Three in One is not to be rejected, merely because it is formally illogical. It relates to a state or continuum in which neither number nor logic holds a meaning. It is, presumably, the best description that our finite minds can compass of a God, who for Christians exhibits Himself as at once the Creator, the Saviour, and the ever-present inspiration of mankind.

The triad seems to convey a truth of profound meaning in the only manner in which the human mind is fitted to receive it. For the Christian it makes of God a companion and friend. For the Hindu the triad represents the Almighty in his aspects of first cause, creator and destroyer. Brahma, Shiva, and Vishnu are severally worshipped in these aspects by the various Hindu sects. The triad figures prominently in some mystical experiences.

It is curious to reflect that scientists who had no other motive than the elucidation of a puzzle of nature, should have stumbled on a truth which is as essential to the interpretation of religion as it is to the interpretation of the physical world. In providing an explanation of the constant velocity of light, they have, at the same time, presented the worshipper with a continuum in which survival may be accepted, not only as a fact, but as a fact which dominates all others in the noumenal and the physical worlds alike.

CHAPTER IV

THE MYSTIC CORROBORATION

In the first three chapters we have considered a point of view which is intended to appeal to persons with scientific sympathies, and a scientific outlook. We showed that life, and not matter, can and should be taken as the basis of the universe, and that life exists as a four dimensional phenomenon. This means that all personalities exist primarily in space-time, and that they exist also in space and time only when they are invested with form.

The importance of the space-time concept is that it is a generalization by which space and time are merged in a further unity. Space and time are the conditions for existence in our three dimensional world of form, motion, and change. Space-time is the condition of existence in general, considered apart from form, motions, and changes of form. The only entity which can, and must, exist in this continuum is life.

Apart from life, we know of nothing which can be regarded as pure existence, and therefore qualified to rank as a purely space-time phenomenon. We have, further, seen that life must be regarded as synonymous with functions that imply life, such as intelligence, purpose, will; also that life can have æsthetic and moral qualities; but no other attributes.

Now many human beings have had experience of existence apart from the body in all ages, and, probably, in all countries. Their testimony about this experience, when it is available, presents features which no man could have invented for himself, and which no number of men separated by time, place and language could have agreed to invent.

It is called the mystic experience.

Its first attribute is the certainty which it imposes on the mind of the mystic. He is absolutely certain that he has seen ultimate reality. In some cases, chiefly drawn from instances of Christian mysticism, he is certain that he has experienced God Himself. The certainty is of a quality that no human knowledge, and no human criticism, can shake.

Its second attribute is that it is supersensual. For this reason it is virtually incommunicable. What the mystic has seen cannot be described in human language, and corresponds to no human thought.

A third attribute is that it is illogical. The mystic is at one and the same time himself and everything else. He experiences a state that knows no forms and no limits. It has no dimensions of space. Time is either felt to be non-existent, or else takes a form which has no correspondence with the time sense of ordinary life.

A fourth attribute is that everything in the mystic experience is intensely alive, and communicates with everything else. The mystic feels that he himself has command of enormously enhanced powers of feeling and perception, and that he is in full communication with every other entity.

All these attributes are such as to be possible attributes of a personality existing apart from the body in space-time. They are so many illustrations of what the state or continuum of space-time must resemble on scientific considerations, when space-time is regarded, as it is in our vital theory, in the capacity of a plenum of life.

The certainty of the mystic arises from the fact that his apprehension in the mystic experience has been extraordinarily vivid. The fact that it is incommunicable is due to the circumstance that it is supersensual. As language is based on sense experience, it follows that language cannot be used to describe something in which sense experience does not enter. It is illogical because human reason is derived from sense experience and cannot deal with a state in which the rules of logic, and the axioms of mathematics, are alike meaningless.

In space-time, time is merged with space, or rather the merger is neither time nor space. So it appears to be to the mystics. In three dimensions time may be best regarded as a dimension, linked with a dimension of space, which represents and measures an ignorance. In the mystic state there is still an ignorance—a possibility of adventure—but it is of a wholly different character from human ignorance.

As we shall see later, when we come to describe the mystic experience in more detail, a second of human time corresponds to a lengthy period of vivid and varied experience in the mystic or, as some people term it, the cosmic state. The feeling that everything is intensely alive, and intelligent in that state, and that the mystic himself is conscious of greatly enhanced powers of feeling and perception, is entirely consonant with the vital theory exhibited in this book.

I conclude that our vital theory, in so far as it is based on ordinary scientific considerations, is in full accord with the mystic report, and that that report operates to confirm the scientific.

I now turn to the evidence. I shall first deal with evidence which relates to mystic states, which have always been recognized as such. It will be seen later that these extraordinary experiences are paralleled by many quite ordinary facts and experiences of our everyday life.

In most cases the state is associated with a certain inhibition of the senses. The most typical cases are nearly always accompanied by inhibition of a very marked kind. There are medical cases in which the experience is associated with an inhibition so complete as to be, medically speaking, all but death. Three or four cases of the kind appear in the proceedings of the Society for Psychical Research. The following account is taken from the *Canadian Tribune*. It was based upon an address delivered in Edinburgh by Lord Geddes (then Sir Auckland Geddes) on the occasion of the Bicentenary of the Royal Medical Society in 1937.

On Saturday, November ninth, a few minutes after midnight, I began to feel very ill, and by two o'clock was definitely suffering from acute gastro enteritis, which kept me vomiting and purging until about eight o'clock. . . . By ten o'clock I had developed all the symptoms of very acute poisoning: intense gastro intestinal pain, diarrhœa—pulse and respirations becoming quite impossible to count. I wanted to ring for assistance, but found I could not, and so placidly gave up the attempt.

I realized I was very ill and very quickly reviewed my whole financial position; thereafter at no time did my consciousness appear to me to be in any way dimmed, but I suddenly realized that my consciousness was separating from another consciousness, which was also me.

These, for the purpose of description, we could call the A and B consciousness, and throughout what follows the ego attached itself to the A consciousness. The B personality I recognized as belonging to the body, and as my physical condition grew worse, and the heart was fibrillating rather than beating, I realized that the B consciousness belonging to the body was beginning to show signs of being composite—that is, built up of consciousnesses from the head, the heart, the viscera, etc. These components became more individual, and the B consciousness began to disintegrate, while the A consciousness, which was now me, seemed to be altogether outside my body, which it could see.

Gradually I realized that I could see not only my body and the bed in which it was, but everything in the whole house and garden, and then I realized that I was seeing, not only things at home, but in London, and in Scotland—in fact, wherever my attention was directed, it seemed to me; and the explanation which I received (from what source I do not know, but which I found myself calling to myself, my mentor), was that I was free in a time dimension of space, wherein now was in some way equivalent to here in the ordinary three-dimensional space of everyday life. I next realized that my vision included, not only things in the ordinary three-dimensional world, but also things in these four or more dimensional places that I was in.

From now on the description is, and must be, entirely metaphorical, because there are no words which really describe what I saw, or rather appreciated. Although I had no body, I had what appeared to be perfect two-eyed vision, and what I saw can only be described in this way: that I was conscious of a psychic stream flowing with life through time, and this gave me the impression of being visible, and it seemed to me to have a particularly intense irridescence.

I understood from my mentor that all our brains are just end organs projecting as it were from the three-dimensional universe into the psychic stream, and flowing with it into the fourth and fifth dimensions. Around each brain, as I saw it, there seemed to be what I can only describe in ordinary words as a condensation of the psychic stream, which was formed in each case as though it were a cloud; only it was not a cloud.

While I was just appreciating this, the mentor, who was conveying information to me, explained that the fourth dimension was in everything in the three-dimensional space, and, at the same time, everything in the three-dimensional space existed in the fourth dimension, and also in the fifth dimension; and I, at the time, quite clearly understood what was meant, and quite understood how "now" in the fourth dimensional universe was just the same, to all intents and purposes, as "here" in a three-dimensional universe. That is to say a four-dimensional being was everywhere in the "now", just as one is everywhere in the "here" in a three-dimensional view of things.

I then realized that I myself was a condensation, as it were, in the psychic stream, a sort of cloud that was not a cloud; and the visual impression I had of myself was blue. Gradually I began to recognize people, and I saw the psychic condensations attached to A, B, C, D, E, F, and to quite a number of men that I know, especially to G. and H.

In addition, I saw that quite a number of people that I know had very little psychic condensation at all attached to them. In addition to those just mentioned, I saw "I" very clearly, and she also gave a visual impression of blueness; A gave purple and dark red; B, pink; D, rather indefinite grey-brown; E, pearly; and F, apricot colour; G was definitely brown. Each of these condensations varied from all the others in bulk, sharpness of outline, and apparent solidity.

Just as I began to grasp all these, I saw A enter my bedroom. I realized she got a terrible shock, and I saw her hurry to the telephone. I saw my doctor leave his patients and come very quickly, and heard him say, or saw him think, "he is nearly gone". I heard him quite clearly speaking to me on the bed; but I was not in touch with the body and could not answer him. I was really cross when he took a syringe and rapidly injected my body with something, which I afterwards learned was camphor.

As the heart began to beat more strongly, I was drawn back; and I was intensely annoyed, because I was so interested, and just beginning to understand where I was and what I was seeing. I came back into the body really angry at being pulled back, and, once I was back, all the clarity of vision of anything and everything disappeared, and I was just possessed of a glimmer of consciousness, which was suffused with pain.

E

It is surprising to note that this dream, vision, or experience has shown no tendency to fade like a dream would fade, nor has it shown any tendency that I am aware of to grow, or to rationalize itself, as a dream would do. I think that the whole thing simply means that, but for medical treatment of a peculiarly prompt and vigorous kind, I was dead to the three-dimensional universe. If this is so, and if in fact the experience of liberation of consciousness in the fourth-dimensional universe is not imagination, it is a most important matter to place on record.

Since my return with the injections, there has been no repetition of any sort or kind of the experience, or of the clear understanding that I seemed to have while I was free from the body.

This example of the cosmic experience is peculiarly valuable for my present purpose. It is modern. It is typical. It resulted from the advent of conditions, which would ordinarily have led to death of the body, and may therefore be presumed to typify what we all must, one day, experience. As a piece of evidence it has all the marks of truth. It could not have been invented. It was recorded without delay, and so forth. I will not here stress the obvious.

Another example which is equally interesting and valuable is that of P. D. Ouspensky, the philosopher, to whom above all others the main reasonings of this book are, either directly or indirectly, due. Some twenty years ago he found the means of inducing in himself the mystic state. He does not tell us the means. Indeed he refuses to do so. We are left to infer that in some way he practised inhibiting his senses, this being the most common way in which the experience is induced. He produced the condition very frequently, and quite deliberately, in order to make scientific observation of its content. He has devoted a chapter in his book called *A New Model of the Universe*, to describing it.

The description is a masterpiece of restrained, but detailed, description. I do not propose to give many details of it here, since, in essentials, it is the experience described in Lord Geddes' paper. It differs mainly, I might almost say only, from that experience in containing a far greater wealth of detail. He achieved a state in which his perceptions and emotions became indefinitely exalted. He was aware of the common things of this life, and notes that they became alive.

Houses, for example, were seen to be living entities, or to consist in living entities. He communicated with the lives making up an ash tray. He spoke, if we can talk of speech without language, with the entities of his own body. He tells us that everything is alive and intelligent, that everything communicates with everything else. Everything is itself and at the same time everything else. There are no forms and no boundaries.

He tried to dictate his experience while in the act of undergoing it, and found that between the words of the simplest sentence he experienced a flood of experience which made it appear that vast periods of time elapsed between them. He was for this reason unable to finish the simplest communication with his assistant. He concludes that one of the marks of the cosmic experience is a fundamentally changed sense of time.

He found that each living entity, or to be more particular, each human being is in the cosmic state the integration of his three-dimensional life. He is what, for this reason, the Hindus call the "long man". He had strange perceptions of infinity.

The infinity pictured in three dimensions as produced by prolongation, and addition, gave place to an infinity produced by repetition without such extension. The number three became strangely significant, and gave him the impression that the universe is built up of triads in shifting mathematical patterns. What we know as motion gave place to intercommunication and interaction between the living entities in which the state consists.

He experienced strange terrors, and strange exaltations. His personality became annihilated, and in turn universal. He felt that his ego was unimportant, and that its highest destiny is absorption in the all. I will not continue a very imperfect, because an impossible, attempt to condense an account, in which no word or sentence is wasted, and in which every word and sentence is essential to the picture which

[67]

results. I have, however, said enough to indicate that what Ouspensky experienced is what Lord Geddes' subject experienced.

The two experiences are virtually identical, except that Ouspensky's account is far more detailed, and that the accounts given by the two men represent slightly different ways of describing what, for each, was essentially indescribable. None the less the two accounts have an essential unity which cannot be questioned.

Now this unity is exactly the feature which makes the mystic experience recognizable in the accounts that have come down to us through the Hindus, the ancient Greek philosophers, other philosophers like Plotinus and Leibnitz, and the great religious prophets and reformers.

For the moment I will pass over the Christian tradition of mysticism. I do so because I wish to keep my account as far as possible in what may be termed the scientific, and philosophic tradition. I also pass over the accounts handed down by the Chinese, the Sufis, the Jews, and others. It is easy to lose oneself in this vast field of human experience of the beyond.

It is essentially the experience of the real behind the phenomenal; and it is essentially incapable of accurate, possibly of any, description. Through it all there looms an account of the real universe, which is the vital universe to which modern science is leading us, and which has been described in preceding chapters.

Parmenides, to whom we have referred in the second chapter, perceived it. So did Plato. His doctrine of ideas is nothing but the perception of the reality behind the phenomenal. His parable of the cave, with which Jeans has familiarized the present generation, is precisely this perception. Plotinus followed in his footsteps, as anyone who takes the trouble to read Dean Inge's account of that philosopher can easily satisfy himself.

Leibnitz's philosophy is simply a repetition of the same perception. I have given a short account of his monadology in the second chapter of this book.

[68]

In none of these cases can the account given be attributed to ordinary three-dimensional experience or reasoning. It is pure revelation.

So far my instances have been drawn from cases, which have either a casual relation to sense inhibition, or possibly no relation at all. Lord Geddes' revenant experienced the type of inhibition we will all experience at death. We do not know how Parmenides, Plato, and Plotinus came by their mystic knowledge.

The same is true of Leibnitz whose metaphysic is substantially that to which, three hundred years later, modern science directly points. His anticipation of the facts, which stamp his philosophy with the seal of scientific truth, is another instance of mystic miracle.

The mystic experience can be deliberately brought about, as we have seen in the case of Ouspensky. The Hindu Yogi takes this course. He puts himself through a course of training, which brings both his mind and his body under an astonishing control.

When he is ready for the trance, he inhibits both from functioning to a degree which often simulates death. In such cases the functions of the body cease, or are so slowed down as to become imperceptible. This is the result achieved by the extreme form of preparation. Some Yogis enter the trance state with far less disturbance of the usual functions; though some degree of inhibition seems to be always present.

The type that we are now discussing has been known to history for some 2,800 years, or, say, since the time of Shankara. Hindus give it a far greater antiquity, running into many thousands of years, on the basis of tradition.

It is discussed in the Vedas, and is the basis of the philosophy which underlies them. It is the basis of the Hindu philosophy of the present day. That philosophy is, to all intents and purposes, one with that which is presented by Ouspensky, and with that which emerges from the writings of Parmenides, Plato, Plotinus, and Leibnitz. It is the vision of the dying man, whose report is produced by Lord Geddes.

It would seem then that the mystic experience in its

more characteristic forms, that is to say in the forms which suggest a philosophy, is generally preceded by some form of asceticism. It requires some inhibition of the normal bodily and mental faculties. It would also seem that the more complete the inhibition, the more vivid the experience. There are exceptions; but on the whole this statement may be accepted as generally true.

It follows that—contrary to all reasonable anticipations—this wonderful awakening and intensification of the emotions and the perceptions takes place precisely when the bodily connection of the mystic with the ordinary world is at its most tenuous. The nearer he is to death, the greater, the more vivid, become his mental and emotional capacities.

It would seem that a man commences to live only when he is at the point of death. This indicates that the life of the human personality is not dependent upon that of the body. The body operates to shackle the dominant personality to a number of other personalities, whose activities interfere with its perception of the real behind the phenomenal world. These personalities are, as we have seen, what the Hindus call the spirits of the body. It will be remembered that both Ouspensky and Lord Geddes' mystic speak of them in this manner.

Death is, evidently, the parting of the dominant personality from those lesser personalities, and operates in the manner of a release from the limitations which they impose on it. There is no evidence that the dominant, or any, personality is ever extinguished. The evidence is all in the direction of survival.

There is a good deal of other evidence which indicates directly that the personality is not dependent on the body, and that it can separate itself from the body, even before the occurrence of death.

Hereward Carrington has given a number of instances in his *Psychic World* (G. P. Putnam's Sons). The relevant chapter is headed *Psychic Phenomena Among Primitive Peoples*. They all point to a power possessed by certain persons of sending their personalities out from their bodies, often to great distances, and utilizing them to observe and bring back news of occurrences, which are later verified, when ordinary means of communication have become available.

Mr. Carrington gives several instances out of which I select the following as typical. A Mr. Bloch (p. 210) tells us that he quarrelled with his partner in Ashanti on a Monday. He left him and travelled light to Cape Coast Castle as rapidly as possible. On arrival there on Saturday, he was told that his partner had died on Wednesday. The news turned out to be true. There was no means of communication, which in the ordinary way could have outstripped the traveller himself. The news of the death arrived in Cape Coast Castle on the day following the death, and two days before Mr. Bloch's arrival.

In this case the person who had projected himself to the place of the death is not named. In a previous story, which relates a similar experience, he is identified as the local magician, who announced that he had obtained it while wandering at a distance of a month's travel away in the shape of a jackal (p. 206). In this case he was able to give news of the approach of a certain accurately described person a month before he arrived, or could have arrived.

These, and many other instances, with which dwellers in the wilds of Africa are familiar, point to the existence of a power of freeing the personality from the body. If this can be brought about during life, it can take place at death. In other words it indicates that the personality is essentially independent of the body.

On this showing, is there any reason why it should die with the body?

A further deduction from this type of experience is that the senses are not essential to perception, even to three-dimensional perception. We can see without eyes, and hear without ears.

On page 206, Mr. Carrington tells us that, in Africa, persons can be, and are, deliberately trained to acquire and use these strange powers. There are similar instances from India, and from the Red Indian tribes in North America.

The instances from India are numerous. I have abstained from utilizing them, because, for my present purpose, the cases drawn from primitive peoples are likely to be more convincing. They are certainly less likely to be fabricated.

Some of my readers may be wondering why I have not rested the case for survival mainly on the evidence provided by the spiritualists. Well, I have certain reasons, none of which are due to a disbelief in the occurrence of spiritualistic phenomena. Of course, neither I nor any other careful person believes in *all* the phenomena reported as spiritualistic.

There is an immense amount of fraud both deliberate, and what may be called accommodatory. Fraudulent persons may seek to make money out of faked phenomena. Even honest mediums, on occasions, may embroider their phenomena with the almost laudable object of not sending an expectant circle away dissatisfied.

Nevertheless, when all allowances have been made, it is now generally agreed that there is a large residuum of genuine spiritualistic experience. This being the case, it follows, or would seem to follow, that survival must be taken as proved. I suppose so. And yet, are the spirits which communicate always the spirits that they pretend to be?

Is there any guarantee that, in raising the spirits of the dead—an ancient procedure, and one that has not always been regarded as creditable—we are not getting in touch with forces that are not only deceiving us, but, are formidable for evil?

Again, are the trivialities, which form the substance of so many communications, worthy of our dead? Granted that they often show a knowledge of facts, which guarantee that the communicating spirit has a strange knowledge of matters—which no one but the departed can be expected to know—are we supposed to infer that in the after-life we may expect to degenerate to the same intellectual level?

Is it not possible that spirits are able to see from their plane all past happenings on ours, so that a communicating spirit has it in his power to assume personalities that do not belong to him? If so, may not certain debased spirits make use of this power in a sort of evil sport?

I do not know. I would feel far more comfortable about spiritualism if the spirits who communicate maintained a higher level in their dealings with mankind.

My feeling is, and I am sure that many share it, that spiritualism does establish the existence of spirits, and, therefore, of survival. The idea that all, or any, of the communicating spirits have never inhabited this earth is too remote to be entertained. It is against all the evidence, and all the probabilities. But whether we ever, or often, get into touch with spirits, who are fulfilling what ought to be the destiny of every human soul, by rising in the scale of being, is a matter about which I am unable to make up my mind.

Nor am I satisfied on evidence of knowledge of facts private to the listener concerned and the deceased person, who is supposed to be identical with the communicating spirit, that the latter is always the personality he pretends to be.

In a subsequent chapter I propose to make reference to a theosophist who appears to have remarkable powers in the direction of tracing the history of a given piece of matter, or, presumably, of a given person, back through historical and earlier time in very great detail. If this power is possible to a personality who is still in the flesh, it would seem that it must be a common attribute of personalities who have passed out of the flesh.

However, I have only dealt with this matter for the sake of completeness. I believe in survival, and therefore I believe in spiritualism and theosophy as being modes in which man can get in touch with the four-dimensional world, and with the personalities that inhabit it. But . . . well; all things are lawful, but all things are not expedient.

It will be understood that my opinion in these matters is given without the backing of any special knowledge or study. It is of the nature of a personal explanation—and apology.

To return to my main line: I would now invite the reader

to consider whether a mystical quality does not appear in men far more commonly that is generally supposed. Hitherto I have only spoken of a type of mysticism which implies a very complete insight into the nature of the world of reality. But, have not all, or nearly all, men intimations of a lesser kind of its existence?

How else are we to account for the almost universal belief in survival in some form? How else are we to account for the comfort that the worshipper derives from prayer; for the sense of spiritual comfort, the experience of help, that he is often conscious of obtaining from it? How are we to account for the fact that the urge to prayer in some form is so nearly universal?

Then take the phenomena of conversion. It is a deep emotional experience, which was so widespread and so uniform, that it must have been based on truth of a cosmic character. In some cases it was felt as a direct perception of God, which was so vivid that the subject was ever after a changed being. The Hindus hold that a man who has had the cosmic experience is henceforth incapable of moral short-coming. In respect of the Christian religion William James has cited many instances of direct revelation which produced the same indelible effect.

Then we have the poets with their sense of "something far more deeply interfused", the musicians with their celestial harmonies, and their hunger to communicate them, the mathematicians with their insight into predetermined harmonies of form and number, the cosmic truth of which is so often confirmed by subsequent physical research and theory.

The relativity theory is based on several such harmonies of pure mathematics. We may dismiss such pehenomena as these rather lightly by attributing them to intuition. The word does not, however, explain anything. On the contrary, by constant and thoughtless use, it serves to cloak the wonders that it classifies.

Is it not possible that intuition is mystical power that practically all men share? Is it not possible that the reasoning process known as induction is an example of this process? If it is not, then, all that there is to say is that it is not otherwise accounted for. It remains what Whitehead has termed it—the despair of philosophers.

It is interesting to consider that every truth that we see, or think that we see, is due to the use of mystic power. It may be more than interesting. It may be true.

Again, the mystic experience in some of the imperfect forms that we have just been discussing, and also in the forms in which it attends purely physical stimuli, does not carry any moral, æsthetic, or intellectual implications. It can be induced by drugs; and there is ancient tradition that it was so induced very anciently by the Hindus. Certain Moslem sects, like the Sufis, are supposed to use the same means.

The modern dope addict notices that, when under the influence of his pet drug, he experiences a changed sense of time, after the fashion noticed and described by Ouspensky. There are cases in which the medical use of drugs for anæsthesia has resulted in producing very remarkable instances of mystic vision.

Some epileptics, again, report that in their seizures they sometimes have an experience of mystic quality. Mystic experiences are not always pleasant experiences. The reader of De Quincey will remember the horrors that attended his opium dreams. The habitual drunkard will confirm him. Even in its purer form the subject often finds that the experience is terrifying in the extreme.

Now all this shows that the mystic experience is, in some degree, a common, possibly a universal, human experience. It means that the real world intrudes on three-dimensional life at many points. It is indeed one of the commonest elements in human life. It is so common that we are inclined to take it for granted.

To sum up the contents of this chapter in respect of its essentials I may point out that there are types of mystic experience which depict reality as a continuum of life—a vital ether.

That ether may be regarded as the inertial field, the

background of reality for which the scientists are seeking, and which the Michelson-Morley experiment failed to find. It is, however, the ether at whose existence the equation of flat space-time, which that experiment has necessitated, hints.

If the equation has a real meaning, its space-time background ought to have a real meaning also. The only real meaning that it can have is that the background, of which we are in search, is one that cannot be detected by physical means. These requirements are exactly those which our vital ether fulfills.

The fact that the more perfect types of the mystic experience depict a continuum of exactly this type is so striking as to be practically conclusive. If we ask science to assume that every entity in the universe from the electron up is a living and intelligent personality—and science should have no objection to an assumption which unifies without disturbing any of its conclusions—then the space-time of science becomes a plenum of life, and, in assuming this aspect, becomes completely assimilated to the mystic continuum or state.

From this position other conclusions emerge.

If every entity is alive and has an existence in space-time as well as in three dimensions, then the onus of proving that there is such a phenomenon as extinction is on the asserter. Death is simply a phenomenon which we associate with the disappearance of a personality from the three-dimensional plane. In other words it is our term for the fact that he is no longer shadowed on that plane.

We have seen, moreover, that at death, or rather when the senses are so inhibited as to produce a simulation of death, the personality is then often to be found at its highest pitch of intellectual and emotional power. This looks as if the complete inhibition of the senses, which we call death, is nothing but a release of the personality from association with the multitude of other personalities, which we call the body. The argument is completed by the evidence on which we have touched, which shows that some persons are able to separate their personalities from their bodies during life.

This is the argument for survival which emerges from our vital theory. It appears to be fairly conclusive.

The spiritualists and the theosophists provide additional and independent evidence, which points in the same direction.

Finally we have been led to wonder whether this mystic experience, which so powerfully reinforces our vital theory, and which fits so well with the conclusions of modern science, is really so exceptional as we are inclined to think it. In its more perfect forms it certainly is exceptional. But, are there not common kinds of fact in human life which appear to have mystical quality? Is not ordinary prayer of an earnest kind a mystical function? Is not human reason, especially reasoning of the kind called inductive, a power which may be thought of as belonging to the mystic class? What are we to say of some of the visions produced at times by anæsthetics and drugs, especially when they reproduce that change in the sense of time, which we have seen to be one of the marks of the true mystic state? What are we to say of the intuitions of the poets, painters, and musicians, of the existence of some wonderful living reality behind the scenes, the colours, the shapes and the sounds, which we meet with in life?

In a later chapter I hope to have something to say about the mystic quality exhibited by religion. Its outstanding importance in this connection entitles it to separate consideration.

CHAPTER V

SIR JAMES JEANS AND HIS CRITICS

THE previous chapters contain in outline an interpretation of the universe based on ideas, which in essence go back to the ancient Greeks, but which have been expressed in more modern form by Leibnitz, who wrote in the time of Newton; and during the last fifty years by many writers of whom Ouspensky, Whitehead, Jeans and Eddington are best known to the writer.

On the purely scientific side Sir James Jeans is perhaps the clearest exponent of the new transcendentalism. It is possibly because of his wide appeal to the educated general public that he has been so extensively and severely criticized by scientists, who disagree with his metaphysical outlook.

There are two main lines along which this attack proceeds. They are inconsistent with each other, but each is fairly virulent.

Bertrand Russell seems to stand alone in accepting Jeans' transcendentalism, while ridiculing its importance. Jeans' interpretation of the universe is consistent with a dignified view of man and his destiny, and it is fairly obvious that this view is intentionally pressed in writings, which are formally based on modern physical theory.

Bertrand Russell, on the other hand, thinks that "the universe is all spots and jumps, without unity, without continuity, without coherence or orderliness or any of the other properties that governesses love. . . . Order, unity, and continuity are human inventions just as truly as are catalogues and encyclopædias. . . . It seems probable that any world, no matter what, could be brought by a mathematician of sufficient skill within the scope of general laws. If this be so, the mathematical character of modern physics is not a fact about the world, but merely a tribute to the skill of the physicists." I requote the passage quoted by Jeans in his *New Background of Science*.

The latter's answer is devastating. It is to the effect that a mathematician might be able to pick out facts showing an orderly sequence from any sort of chaos; but the sequences evolved by this process would be useless for the purpose of prediction. The fact that predictions can be, and are, successfully based on the facts, as they exist, suffices to disprove Russell's view.

It appears to me that Russell has omitted to notice that mathematicians are also a part of the universe, hence, if we concede that their thoughts are orderly, we must also concede at least this amount of order to the universe. Even Russell might agree that mathematicians are not the only human beings whose thoughts are orderly.

His cynical view of the universe rings false. If it were really like Gilbert's *Wandering Minstrel*, "a thing of shreds and patches," the survival of the human race would have been impossible. It is hardly necessary to point out that that survival has depended on the observance of a certain orderliness in its societies. The same consideration applies even to animals.

It is queer to reflect that, whereas the older cynics of yesterday based an unhappy view of the universe on a supposed excess of order of the mechanical variety, the modern cynic comes to a similar conclusion by exaggerating its disorder.

I will not consider further a view which seems to be based more on temperament than on thought. In my opinion it owes its celebrity to the genius of its author.

The second line of attack does not question the opinions of those who adopt a transcendental view of the universe. It proceeds by denying the right of anyone to base any philosophy on any scientific concept or conclusion. The philosopher materialist of the last century had no right to base his intepretation of the universe on the mechanistic model, which the then known facts thrust upon the scientists.

The transcendentalist of the present day is similarly forbidden to think that modern physics supports his opinions. This, according to the school of thought that we are now considering, holds true throughout the whole of the age which has seen the development of science on its present lines.

The appearance of impartiality presented by this attitude is only an appearance. Materialism made a deep impression on human thought, and that impression has largely survived the very recent proof that it has no basis. The textbooks of the social and biological sciences are more often than not written against a materialistic background. Medicine, as Carrel ably shows, is under the same handicap. Its reliance on a mechanistic view of the human body has produced dangers, which are characteristic of that view, and which are very menacing.

The teachers of the young also are largely inclined to adopt a view of the universe, which, if it has not the merit of being true, has at least the merit of being easy.

It follows that the only practical alternative to a transcendental form of philosophy, which may be true, is a materialistic philosophy, which is certainly untrue. Thus, by denying any philosophy the right to base itself on science, the scientists, whom we are discussing, are condemning their generation to continue to believe in a philosophy which is now admitted by them to be falsely based.

This is, however, by the way. The school we are discussing bases itself on a dogma known as operationalism. A statement to have scientific value must be based on observable facts, and must state the means by which its truth can be verified by experiment. If it complies with these requirements it is "operational". As, in the opinion of the operationalists, no metaphysical statement can comply with them, the gap between science and philosophy becomes unbridgeable.

This rather pompous dogma can be expressed in much more homely terms. It amounts to no more than the adage which states that the proof of the pudding is in the eating. I do not like to insist on the rider that scientists are apparently the only people who are allowed to eat the scientific puddings, and they are condemned to eat nothing else.

Scientific statements based on the known facts have always complied with the operational requirements. This is as true of the statements made by Newton as of the statements made by the relativists and quantum physicists of our own day. The trouble is that in past times scientific statements were too often seized on by the metaphysicians and recast in the form of concepts.

Thus a statement about, shall we say, gravitation, made in a form of scientific value, became popularized as a "law" of gravitation. It became a "law of Nature". Men came to picture the universe as being controlled by those idealized concepts parading as natural laws.

I think we may take it that the day in which errors of this nature were possible is past. It is certainly past for science. It is difficult to imagine men like Jeans, or Eddington, mistaking the mathematical recipes for prediction, which are all that modern physics aspires to produce, for laws.

People, who have no scientific training, may still be in a fog about the nature of what they will no doubt persist in calling laws of Nature; but the operationalists do not profess to cater to them.

The truth is that, in tilting against concepts like those of causation and free will, the operationalists are tilting against windmills. They are also failing to perceive that the basis of modern physics has ceased to be physical. It is a fact that as scientists we know nothing about the nature of causation. It is whatever controls the action of the primary particles. It may be magic for aught we can tell. We are debarred from this knowledge because we are unable to follow the actions of these particles as individuals with

F   [81]

sufficient accuracy. That has been settled by the indeterminacy principle.

The physicist is in much the same position as a reporter of a tennis match, whose sight is too weak to enable him to distinguish between the server and the striker. In much the same way the physicist's apparatus can never enable him to see whether the electron, which starts an interaction, is the electron which emerges from it. He is, in other words, in the position of being unable to identify any given electron.

Under these circumstances he can deal only with their conduct in the mass. His formulæ for prediction are precisely analogous to the tables on which a life insurance company bases its estimates of the duration of the lives of its clients. It is probable that no individual client has ever died in exact accord with the prediction of an insurance table.

It is also probable that no particle has ever behaved in exact accord with the physicist's formula. If it did, he would never be aware of the circumstance. This fact gives an appearance of exactitude to the physicist's predictions, which may be exaggerated.

The physicist has evidence of the existence of the electron; but he does not know what it is like. He does not even know that it is a physical entity. Its presence is deducible from the phenomena it produces when it interacts with its surroundings. But we cannot deduce from this that it is itself physical. A physical fact ought to be a fact which can be perceived by our senses either directly or, indirectly, by the aid of instruments which enlarge the scope of our senses. In this sense, at any rate, the electron for a certainty is not physical.

There is, however, a more fundamental reason for coming to the same conclusion. This takes us to the consideration of the Michelson-Morley experiment on light. It was undertaken to establish the speed of the earth through the ether. It resulted in proving that there is no ether which is discoverable by any method of physical approach. It showed that light has a constant velocity under whatever circumstances it may be measured. It is the same for observers approaching and leaving the source. It is the same whether the source is approaching, or leaving, the observer.

This necessitated the construction of an equation involving the three space co-ordinates and the time variable, which gives the value of a quantity called the interval. The interval is four dimensional, being based on four variables.

The equation shows that there is no fundamental distinction between space and time; but that both are created by our minds from a matrix that merges and contains them both. Each intelligence divides the matrix in accordance with the state of its motion.

An intelligence on the sun will locate a given phenomenon, say, a given star, differently in space and time from us. If there are intelligences in the heavenly bodies in general, there will then be an infinite number of ways in which the space-time matrix is divided into space and time. All these intelligences will, however, arrive at the same value for the interval.

The interval is, as it were, the measure of the separateness of the happenings in the basic continuum, in which space and time are fully merged, that is to say in space-time. The happenings in space-time result from the activities of the entities which inhabit it. They are called events to distinguish them from the phenomena to which they give rise, when they are projected on to our world of space and time. Thus the event is the four dimensional original of the phenomenon. How an event comes to translate itself into a phenomenon is utterly mysterious. We may say, if we like, that it happens by magic.

But, and this is the point which the operationalists have failed to note, this means that the basis of our phenomenal world is not physical. We may call it metaphysical. It seems queer to reflect that what we call the real world that surrounds us is no more than the shadow of a world which is fundamentally much more real. To us the shadow is more real than the substance; but that is only because our senses are not adapted to perceiving the substance.

We may go further and say that we cannot even reason about the space-time continuum, since reason cannot deal with what the mind cannot picture. All this means that a strictly "operational" experiment has led to an "operational" assertion that the physical is based on the nonphysical. It means that science has become transcendental from the base up. It is no longer based on observable facts.

The operationalists ought to see that, if they accept the modern position about space-time (and they do accept it), they must base themselves, as scientists, on a metaphysical concept.

In this connection we may use the word concept without offence, since it stands for the statement that whatever is behind phenomena cannot be called physical.

What modern science has done is to drive our ideas of causation back into the realm of the nonphysical. Causation, being linked with the problem of free will, that matter, too, must be relegated to the unknown possibilities of space-time. Causation and free will alike become first causes and, as such, are incapable of being "explained" in terms of anything else. Also they become incapable of being defined. Presumably the two words are synonyms for the same thing.

Thus, the effect of modern physics is to provide both the philosopher and the scientist with a common starting point, and to bridge the gap which the operational dogma regards as being unbridgeable.

Another gap, which appears to be on the way to being bridged by modern physics, is that between the animate and the inanimate. The four-dimensional, which appears to be so mysterious, may be merely the mental. Our minds may be familiar examples of four dimensional entities, and their operations examples of four-dimensional activities. The same may be true of the primary particles.

They, too, may be intelligent entities. So may all their combinations; and the combinations in question may be examples of the piling of personality on personalities in a complex process at the head of which we humans stand.

Bertrand Russell appears to be ready to accept some such position, and I imagine that scientists like Sir James Jeans and Sir Arthur Eddington would agree with him. These possibilities are however at the moment rather beyond the scope of recognized scientific thinking. The operationalists are, of course, debarred by their primary dogma from thinking about them at all.

A great deal of a book like that written on the operational side by Philipp Frank, entitled *Between Physics and Philosophy*, is taken up with attacks on positions that have already been by-passed. He is severe on metaphysical ideas of causation; whereas, as we have seen, the whole basis of causation in the modern view is nonphysical. That is to say it must be regarded as metaphysical. Basically considered, quantum physics is inseparable from metaphysics.

The same author spends several pages on combating the view, advanced by some philosophers, that the principle of indeterminacy affords a basis for believing in free will. But, as we have seen, free will, being linked with our theories about causation, being in fact an aspect of causation, cannot be defended or attacked in isolation.

If causation is a sort of first cause, a fundamental mystery from which everything flows, but which is itself unintelligible, then we must relegate the free-will problem to the same origin. If we know nothing about causation, we are for this very reason in a state of similar ignorance about free will.

Sir James Jeans points out that the wave theory of the primary particles includes the principle of indeterminacy in a wider sweep, and that the basis of the wave theory is our inability to observe, or otherwise estimate, the behaviour of the primary particles, except in the mass. The theory is a formal admission of our ignorance of what causation may be, or may mean.

Although this chapter was written primarily as a defence of Sir James' attitude towards the philosophical implication of modern physics, I find that I have said very little about it. As a matter of fact I have endeavoured to adopt it throughout this book in so far as the context permits me to do so. If I have misrepresented it, I trust that he will not judge the attempts of a layman too strictly.

There is, however, one point which I would like to discuss before closing this chapter.

It concerns the part played by time in the new philosophy. Sir James accepts space-time in its most general form, in which the four variables are indistinguishable, as the basic truth of the physical universe. In this form, however, time is completely merged with space to form the basic continuum. But, if this is the case, what importance are we to assign to human history, and how are we to interpret that part of relativity physics which deals with the molar masses?

The difficulty may be made more evident when we consider that the primary space-time equation has two forms. One is the universal form already referred to. The other shows the time element associated with a negative sign and the square of the relative velocity of the "observer". In this form it has a domestic aspect. It is one of a possible infinity of space and time aspects of the cosmos; but, as it is our aspect, it has a peculiar interest and importance for us. It will have none for intelligences which do not use it.

A book might be filled with speculations about the extent to which each of the various human activities deals, or does not deal, with the cosmic, as opposed to the domestic, aspect of human life.

The examples I have suggested are only examples. Human history has great interest and importance for human beings, and the fact that a record of the happenings of the past, on our three dimensional plane, is unlikely to have much meaning when we pass beyond it, need not trouble us.

For the believer in an after-life the importance of all human activity lies rather in the spirit in which it is undertaken, than in its historical consequences. For those who do not believe in survival the distinction between the cosmic and the domestic varieties of the space-time equation is unmeaning.

In molar physics the use of the domestic variety is compulsory. Here our mathematicians are compelled to handle the four primary variables by contrasting one of them with the other three. The only variable which lends itself to this process is that which directly involves the time element. It is used as the basis of a picture in which space is represented as being drawn through time.

On this basis our physicists can make a mathematical representation of space-time, which pictures the molar masses as being centres of curvature, while being themselves of the nature of higher curvatures. The curvatures are geodesics along which lie the past and predicted paths of every assembly of matter. Light in its travel from a star is bent around the curvatures it meets on its way to our eyes, or telescopes.

This introduces an element of uncertainty into the estimates of astronomic distances based on the travel of light. It is, moreover, an element which cannot be allowed for by averaging or any other process, since we do not know what bodies and what curvatures have been encountered in given instances.

When we come to discuss the apparent speeds of recession of the nebulæ, and to deduce from them theories of expanding or contracting universes, our speculations approach the fantastic. They are the more fantastic when we reflect that they centre round an unreal separation of the time element from the other ingredients of the space-time equation.

And yet . . . well, they are not altogether fantastic. They are logical extensions of the reasoning which has produced the calculations and data by which our ships are guided on the seas, and by which we undertake the highly practical business of obtaining accurate measures of the lapse of time.

In their more recent form they provide a very fair correspondence with the evidence of the geological record. On these grounds it is fair to deduce that time has a reality, which is greater than appears to be justified by a strict reading of the basic space-time equation.

The same conclusion might be reached on more general

grounds. If we hold that space-time is the habitat of every entity that exists, and that the said entities are alive, intelligent, and purposeful, then there is an infinity of space and time universes, in each of which we must suppose that time plays a part analogous to that which it plays in our reading of the cosmos. We can hardly suppose that the continuum in which space and time are fully merged is available to any intelligence other than that of the Creator.

In the above speculation I have based myself on Sir James' very sagacious hint that time may have a more fundamental meaning than a strict interpretation of the generalized space-time equation would justify. It is curious that the difficulty we have been discussing should arise only on the molar side of human experience.

It does not appear in the wave theory of quantic physics. This may be because, in that theory, no attempt is made to deal with observations on individual particles. In astronomy, of course, the individual star or nebula is considered under conditions which often approach the limit of our powers of observation. This means that we are near the point at which shadow and substance meet in the mystical, or transcendental, sense already alluded to.

In that sense, what is real for physics is but a portion of a higher and more deeply interfused reality, which physics cannot deal with, but which it is now compelled to recognize as a fact.

It is the business of philosophy to get behind the meaning of words, more especially of words that denote classifications. Our vital theory is an example of this. It seeks to show that the obvious and practical necessity for distinguishing the animate from the inanimate, the organic from the inorganic, life from death, has been pressed too far, and that, so pressed, it has led to a fundamentally erroneous concept. May not the concept of time be similarly misleading?

Where human experience is concerned with sensory phenomena the idea of time always involves duration. Apart from the measured durations of the day, the month, the year, and so forth, it is evident that our every physical act also implies time in its guise (or disguise) of duration. To consider the simple example of walking, it is self-evident that each step is a duration.

With this hint the reader can furnish himself with a profusion of verifications of the proposition that the concept of time in connection with sensory experience (actual or imagined) always implies durations.

I may note here that this type of experience is also conditioned by another factor. There is a spatial order which rules the physical universe. It may be very simply indicated by the statements that I cannot leave the room without walking to the door, opening it, and stepping out: similarly I cannot go from New York to London without crossing a body of water.

It will be noted that the duration aspect of time and, what I have called, the spatial order are always present together. This means that our sensory experience is clogged by conditions, which, in the case of the time element, make time a synonym for duration.

But, if we suppose with the mystics, and in accordance with the vital theory, that there is a four-dimensional life ahead of us, in which sense experience with its durations and spatial order ceases to exist, time can only mean or refer to experience that is free from those clogs.

In that life, time will no longer be synonymous with duration because the conditions under which durations arise will not exist. It will then stand out as a condition of experience or, preferably, as experience itself. It will be, in other words, a term denoting the personality in action. From this point of view, and for the continuum in which sensory experience is non-existent, time is experience.

The point we are making enables us to reconcile two apparently contradictory statements about time which occur in accounts of the mystic experience. Some mystics describe it as one in which the sense of time is utterly changed. Others describe it as timeless.

It is evident that it is timeless, if time is regarded as synonymous with duration, as is the case for the world of physical experience with which the contrast is made. Space is the concept under which we classify the impact of crowds of photons on our nerve centres, after our minds have transformed the process into mental images. The crowds must in every case be dense enough to pass the threshold of sensation. Sir James stresses this very important point.

A crowd is impersonal and, in this, is in marked contrast to the individuals that compose it. The latter are always personalities. It follows that our sensory experience is always experience of impersonal aspects of Nature. From another point of view it is experience of averages, and not of the realities, the individual facts, on which the averages are based.

CHAPTER VI

EDDINGTON'S PHYSICS, A FORM OF MYSTICISM

RELIGION and science figure prominently in these pages. Indeed our object is to show that they now supplement each other, and combine to present an explanation of man's place and function in the universe. Sir Arthur Eddington's latest book, *The Philosophy of Physics*, is intended to show the place of physics in the general scheme of thought and of the universe.

On the one hand, it tends to restrain exaggerated claims on the part of science to answer all the questions that man can ask and, on the other, it clarifies the nature of the process by which physics answers the questions that properly fall within its domain.

I am considering it here because it provides one of the latest and most authoritative expositions of the metaphysical status of a branch of research that has assumed spectacular importance, and also because its conclusions fortify those with which I am mainly concerned.

It is difficult reading for the non-technical reader. The writer shares his difficulty, and begs in advance indulgence for such misapprehensions as may arise from his want of mathematical and technical equipment.

To begin with it may be stated that Sir Arthur takes his stand on a fairly simple view of the universe out of which physics has carved the domain with which his book is concerned. It is the view adopted in the preceding chapters.

There is a reality behind the shapes, sounds, colours and motions with which our senses present us and which, through the medium of the senses, our minds transform. As will be seen later, physics refuses to consider it for very excellent reasons. We have, of course, regarded it as life.

Then, Sir Arthur believes in the "real" existence of other people. He regards our evidence for their existence as a sort of sympathetic knowledge. Our evidence for the existence of our fellow men is stronger than our evidence for the existence of what may be roughly described as matter. This is because our fellow men can influence us in ways that are impossible to matter in a three-dimensional world. Thus Sir Arthur, like ourselves, starts with a phenomenal world based on a core of mysterious reality, and containing intelligences which co-operate in examining it.

Physics is concerned with our apprehension of that world in the aspects which they, as a fact, consider physical. In order to avoid refinements that are not essential to our understanding of his position, we may call them its commensurable aspects. They are the aspects which lend themselves to quantitative examination, and which can be used to check the exuberance of human theories about the physical universe. In a word they are what may be termed the physical facts.

Sir Arthur commences with the proposition that those facts are for the physicist mental facts, since they consist in the translations made by our minds of the messages conveyed to them by the senses. All knowledge for the physicist is mental knowledge. He does not deny the possibility of other knowledge; but he is not concerned with it.

On this basis, which I hope that I have explained correctly, he proceeds to analyse the content of physical knowledge with special reference to its modern developments.

Until the end of the last century physicists were prone to translate their knowledge in terms of pictures. Newton conceived of a mysterious entity called force, and laid down the laws of its operation, in a manner which revolutionized man's outlook on the universe.

Then came the picture of the ether. It was assumed to exist as the medium by which light is carried across space by means of wave motions defined by certain mathematical equations. Later, this concept was extended to cover all electro-magnetic waves, whether visible or invisible. They were all supposed to be carried by the same ether.

Before the atom was split, it was conceived of as the ultimate division into which a particle of an element could be divided without ceasing to be that element. It was pictured as a sort of tiny sphere. It was also assumed that it represented the ultimate entity of the inorganic creation.

Later, as we all know, it was found that the atom is made up of electrons, protons, and neutrons, but for the sake of brevity we shall frequently describe the atom as made up of electrons and protons. Bohr's celebrated, and still serviceable, theory pictured it as a sort of tiny planetary system, in which the electrons revolve round a nucleus. On this theory, electrons and protons were substituted for atoms as the ultimate material of the world.

In the course of the last forty years each and all of these concepts have been abandoned, and the manner in which this revolution has come about is the main theme of Sir Arthur's philosophy.

He shows how, one after the other, each picture of the ultimate constituents of the universe has become misleading, and how, after its abandonment, further progress became possible without making alternative pictures.

It has become more and more a series of mathematical statements about the conduct of entities such as protons, electrons and photons, those entities being represented as existing in no more picturable form than that of mathematical symbols. The resulting equations have no other justification than that supplied by experiment and observation; and this justification suffices.

As a matter of fact the symbolic universe so depicted is even more a mental creation than our sketch indicates. This follows from the fact that science no longer deals with even a supposed individual electron, proton, or photon. It recognizes that these ultimates have no distinguishable individualities. We do not know in a given case whether we are dealing with electron A or electron B, and our mathematics have to be constructed so as to recognize this limitation.

Further still, the conduct of the ultimate elements is

pictured, not as necessary conduct, but as probable conduct. This has been dealt with in Chapter II. Thus the individual electron, proton, or photon fades completely out of the picture; if picture is still a term which has any relation to the symbolism of modern physics. An average is a number. It has no dimensions and therefore no ascertainable habitation of any kind of space. The numbers which emerge from wave equations appear to stand for probable configurations or structures, which are going through a process of continuous change.

At least this is the mathematical picture, but, since that picture relates not to actual entities but to probabilities, the only human aspect that emerges is that the result given by the equations should be capable of being checked by physical observation.

This is the sole circumstance that keeps the processes of modern quantum physics in touch with what the ordinary man calls reality.

In order to maintain further touch with what we must call reality, physics has discussed the kind of space in which the primary vibrants—the electrons, protons, and photons— have their being. It is presumably a refinement of the space-time of molar physics. But the connection has not been made.

The latest, or one of the latest, refinements in this direction is the so-called Hilbert space—a space of infinite dimensions. I presume, as far as an uninstructed person like myself may make any presumptions in these difficult matters, that the inhabitants of this (or any) space are the ultimate vibrants, which can neither be observed with useful accuracy nor otherwise identified.

As a result, the common-sense world of nineteenth century physics has been resolved into numbers and configurations, based on units whose nature is neither known nor is capable of being known. These units are the electrons, protons and photons, and possibly other ultimates.

The physical world is wholly mental, subject to the condition already mentioned, that the predictions arising from the mathematics can be checked by experiment. Judged by this test they generally emerge triumphant.

Deep down behind the test, and behind the minds which have devised it, lies the core of reality which physics can never reach. We have termed it life.

It will be seen that the picture thus presented has several points in common with the mystic picture. The failure of every attempt to give the ultimate entities the attribute of form, and the fact that those entities are indistinguishable from each other, reminds us of the mystic position in which the one is all and the all one. It agrees with the mystic statement that in the cosmic state form is absent. It strikingly illustrates Ouspensky's description of that state as being made up of mathematical relations.

If indeed the physicists ever succeed in reducing the elementary entities to three—namely electrons, protons and photons—then Ouspensky's statement that the cosmic continuum is a sort of web in which the triad repeats itself indefinitely, and underlies every combination, has a very striking relevance.

One of the most powerful mathematical instruments for dealing with the problems of the new physics is what is known as the theory of groups. It is based on sets of triangular relations as the groundwork of quantic structures. The triad again.

The changed sense of time is an established element in the cosmic experience. In physics we have a parallel phenomenon. In the time scale of atomic physics a hundredth of a second is virtually an eternity. "A characteristic must be 'everlasting' if it is to appear at all in the time-scale of ordinary human perception." Again, pure mysticism. Once more, we have seen that the old idea of force has been given up.

Eddington tells us that "the effect (of indistinguishability) is equivalent to that which would be produced by physical forces of interaction. . . . There is now strong reason to believe that all interaction forces in physics arise from the indistinguishability of the ultimate particles." Interaction has therefore a subjective "origin".

Well, our vital theory attributes the reality behind force and motion to the presence and interactions of personalities in space-time. This is virtually the mystic position. Its agreement with the most modern scientific view is nothing short of amazing. Everything in modern research into the physical side of the universe points ultimately to that

> *Secret Presence that through Nature's veins,*
> *Running like quicksilver eludes our pains,*
> *Taking all shapes from Mah to Mahi, and*
> *These change and perish; only He remains. . . .*

Life is that secret presence, and it presupposes God.

I now turn to the molar side of science—the side that deals with matter in the gross. Here relativity is the modern contribution to scientific knowledge.

Considered from the angle of philosophy, it presents several of the most salient features of the quantum side which we have been considering.

The older scientists considered the existence of the luminiferous ether a certainty. They even calculated the strength of the ether gale that should be observed as blowing over the earth, when the development of suitable apparatus should bring its detection within the range of achievement. As we have seen, the apparatus was devised, but neither the gale nor the ether could be found. We discovered, in its stead, that the velocity of light is constant, and that the familiar concepts of space and time must give way to the further generalization of space-time.

In its turn space-time introduced us to a "real" world in which form and motion became the shadows of mysterious, but real, happenings.

Einstein demolished the familiar concepts of force, as it is envisaged in Newtonian physics, and, in addition, pointed out that the then universally accepted idea of simultaneity is without basis. On these foundations he erected his two theories of relativity.

As we have seen, they reduce the "law" of gravitation to

an equation which deals with a four-dimensional universe and makes the motions of the heavenly bodies result from mathematical curvatures in that continuum.

The curvatures are of course mathematical pictures of the conditions depicted by the equations. Their reality is merely mental.

The equations do not lay down a law of any kind to "govern" the paths of the heavenly bodies. They do no more than describe those paths, and enable us to predict them by suitable calculation. The planets and stars, that is to say the molar bodies themselves, are similarly viewed as higher curvatures.

The processes of the heavens thus become unimaginable processes, taking place in the unimaginable (though real) continuum of space-time.

When it comes to a question of actually calculating the path of a given body, space-time has to be projected on to our ordinary terrestrial time and space.

Incidentally, the relativity theories have necessitated a complete alteration in our ideas of time, space, matter, momentum, energy, location, and other concepts which, until their arrival, were held to be commonplaces of scientific truth.

As in atomic physics, molar physics has now reduced all, or nearly all, of our old pictorial representations of the workings of Nature to an affair of mathematical equations in four dimensions. The old pictures are replaced by symbols and the processes, which the pictures were supposed to represent, by mathematical solutions. Thus, from this direction also, the universe has been reduced to mathematical configurations, or structures, which undergo continuous changes in an unpicturable medium.

We have learned, incidentally, that there is not, and cannot be, any picture of the universe that has absolute truth. Whatever picture we may make from one point of view—that is to say from one state of motion—is unlike that which another state of motion would produce; and both pictures are equally "true".

Although the results of the acceptance of relativity and

G [97]

quantum theories has been to make the processes of Nature infinitely mysterious, and difficult to grasp, yet, viewed from the aspect of practical utility, the progress made has been enormous. The mathematical representation of Nature has justified itself many times over.

But, the world, or rather the universe in its new scientific dress, has evaporated into an affair of mathematical symbols and equations, operating against a mystical background in which both time and space have lost their separate existences.

The molar world, like the world of the atom, has become wholly subjective, with the sole condition that scientific prediction has still to be judged by the test of fact. Our prediction that Mercury will be at a certain place at a certain time must still be verifiable, by observation of its position at the time specified.

In most cases verification has become needless. In this connection it is interesting to realize that we have to adopt in theory a scheme of measurement of space and time which is itself independent of measurement. For this purpose we now use the numbers which represent an atomic lattice in space and in time respectively. The atomic structure gives the numbers for space measurement and the vibrations give the unit for the measure of time.

Here, as in atomic physics, our ultimate units are mere numbers. They must be mere numbers, if they are to be kept independent of the configurations and structures to which they are to be applied.

Thus on the molar side we are once more reduced to a highly mystical point of view. The mystery of space-time is, as we have seen in earlier chapters, the basic mystery of the cosmic experience. Existences in this strange state or condition lose all the attributes, with which we invest them when we view them through the familiar medium of space and time. On both the molar and the atomic scales forces and motions become functions of strange mathematical processes of which we can form no picture. This again is the mystical teaching, or, perhaps we should say, is a natural corollary of that teaching.

Mathematical thought has even attacked, or, shall we say has reformed the processes of our reason. Boule reduced its operations to an algebra, and the theory of groups has extended the process. It has resulted in giving us a subjective mathematical universe in which there are mysterious constants. It is a universe in which the number of atoms in existence can be definitely stated.

Although no one can check this result, it appears to rest on foundations that, in other directions, stand the test of observational attack. It may therefore be accepted as corresponding to something in the still unknown nature of things. From our point of view it should correspond with some aspect of the vital universe.

My technical equipment does not qualify me to discuss these amazing developments. I feel when I read of them, and try to appreciate their general scope, as if I were sitting at "magic casements opening on the foam"—the structural foam of a subjective universe. Once more, from the mystic point of view, a better description of that universe could hardly be given. The Hindu *maya* is not exactly illusion. It is exactly what I have stated.

Sir Arthur stresses the fact that science, especially physical science, is dominated by a desire to reduce its fundamental facts to as small a number as possible. *If* we may take it that physical science has reduced or may reduce its fundamentals to three—electrons, protons, and photons—the further efforts of physicists will centre round attempts to reduce them still further; until final attainment of the ideal leaves us with one fundamental unit, which can be regarded as the source of all the others.

I am not sure that this search will ever be rewarded. The simplest closed area is that which is enclosed by a triangle, and the simplest pattern or structure is therefore based on the triad. It may well be that, after three primary entities have been established, no further progress along lines which depend on structural concepts is possible. However, I must leave this to the experts concerned.

The point I want to make here is that, after the fundamental entities have been established, that is to say after physicists are satisfied that the maximum degree of unity has been attained, we are no nearer the reality behind phenomena. It is common ground with all physicists and all philosophers, who are not solepsists, that there is such a reality.

For physics it is represented by the possibility of checking physical theory against physical observation. Having reduced the fundamental entities to their utmost limit—their utmost mathematical limit—we are left with this as our sole means of keeping in touch with a reality, which must be supposed to exist, but which is not physical. It is not physical because it cannot be detected by physical means.

At this point physics can proceed no further. Its only recourse will be to re-examine the old ground. I have indicated that this course has been, and will most certainly be, very fruitful.

It will then be dealing with a well-defined, but very limited, universe which is based on numbers. The numbers will stand for the probabilities governing the recurrence of mathematical structures. In other words, the world of physics will be an almost wholly mathematical world, which does not profess to have any connection with the ordinary world, except in the fact that its theories can be tested by observation.

Compare this concept with the mystic account. It is practically a replica of Ouspensky's report of the content of the mystical experience.

We have pointed out that the mystic philosophy supports modern science. We now see that the support is reciprocal, and that science is well on the way to reproducing the mystic continuum in its section of the universe.

I gather that Sir Arthur defines physics as what physicists think it is. But this limitation, if it is a limitation, is not rigid.

Present day physics evidently confines itself to matters which are susceptible to some kind of observational test. Its "laws" to be physical laws or physical regularities must be capable of being put to the test of this kind of proof.

We all remember the various expeditions that were sent out to decide whether the Einsteinian prediction of the bending of light is, or is not, confirmed by the facts of observation. The confirmation afforded by the data collected by these expeditions had the effect of placing the Einsteinian theory of gravitation in the rank of what we must call a law.

In other words, it established that the Einsteinian method of calculating the phenomena of gravitation, and with it the far-reaching conception of the processes of the molar universe on which the relativity theory rests, are reliable explanations of the matters to which they refer. The fact that the explanation does not explain, but merely provides a practical alternative to what had previously passed as explanation, emphasizes the distinction between the new view of what constitutes physical law and the old.

But from this new view of law—the view that law is simply a reliable formula for prediction of the conduct of Nature in the sphere with which physics concerns itself— we pass into a wholly new type of thought. We no longer assert that there is some inner compulsion in Nature which guarantees that the prediction will always come off. We assert no more than that it covers the known facts, and may be expected to cover such new facts as may from time to time be ascertained.

When we come to consider atomic physics the contrast between the old and the new points of view becomes still more marked. "The laws which never shall be broken" of the old hymn give place to laws which are never wholly obeyed. This follows from the fact that the new laws are statistical in nature, and rest on a basis of probability. They represent average conduct which is not supposed to be exactly reproduced in any given instance.

The distinction is that between a law that is never broken, and a law that represents a practical certainty, when the limitations of our powers of observation are taken into account. The practical certainty may not, in fact it is not, always realized, but the divergences are either too small to be detected, or else take place too seldom to be detected.

It is, I think, along the line of pursuing the more probable divergences that future progress in atomic physics may be expected. There are indications that this line of inquiry is in fact being opened up.

Thus, a given substance, say salt, under particle bombardment of a given type and strength yields a certain proportion of short time units that are radio-active. Under a bombardment of a different strength the proportion is altered, and the radio-active elements have a different average period of disintegration. As far as the chemist can tell the new radioactive particles differ from their fellows only in the fact that they turn out to be radio-active.

The process, in fact, provides a means for manufacturing new elements without limit. But it is plain that what bombardment operates on is differences in the constitution of the atoms which make up the sample that is submitted to it. In other words the atoms of an element can no longer be regarded as absolutely uniform. They must be regarded as being almost infinitely variable.

The fact that our chemists cannot detect the variations is no longer a guarantee that they do not exist. They do exist, whether they can be detected or not. Phenomena of this kind provide as good proof as we can expect of the vital theory. Spontaneous variation is one of the best tests of the presence of life that we can have.

It would seem to follow that research along the lines of variation must ultimately become identified with a new type of biophysics, which starts with the assumption that everything is alive from the electron up. It will, in short, start with assuming that our vital theory is the only basis of research into the phenomena of variation.

Eddington comes very close to this position. He suggests that:

. . . when we succeed in making progress with the study of the objective world, the result will be very different from present day physics. We have spoken of this as a development in the future; but may it not have occurred already? It seems to me that the "enlarged" physics, which is to include the objective as well as the subjective, is just science; and the objective. which has no reason to conform to the pattern of systematization that distinguishes present day physics, is to be found in the nonphysical part of science. . . . The purely objective sources of the objective element of our observational knowledge have already been named; they are life, consciousness, spirit. . . . The purely objective world is the spiritual world; and the material world is subjective in the sense of selective subjectivism.

All that this needs to make it coincide with our vital theory is the identification of the terms life, consciousness, spirit as synonyms for the underlying reality.

CHAPTER VII

DE REBUS QUIBUSDAM ALIIS

THE previous chapters have been directed to providing proof of the falsity of the current materialism, and to showing that survival of the personality in a continuum, which may be identified with the space-time of the physicists, is to be expected. The proof has proceeded on the line of showing that space-time, as specified by the mathematician, is precisely the continuum which the mystics have experienced all down the ages in their characteristic trance.

There are confirmations of this position, which have either been neglected, so far, or have been very inadequately mentioned. The important theosophic branch of research, which has become very active, has not been mentioned at all. This is because I have had practically no knowledge of it until quite recently.

I fear that such knowledge as I have recently acquired is of the most sketchy description; but so far as it goes it appears to me to provide striking confirmation of the general argument of this book.

A great deal of the theosophic research to which I have referred relates to obtaining details of, what I have called, the space-time experience, but which in theosophic terminology appears to be called the astral plane, or planes.

I learn that there are people who have the power of entering the space-time or astral state at will. It is a part of their normal make-up. One of these clairvoyants, a Mr. Geoffrey Hodson, has collaborated with a Mr. Alexander Horne in writing a book on the subject of certain experiments which they jointly conducted for the purpose of ascertaining details about the space-time continuum, or, as they would term it, the etheric and astral planes. The title of the book is *Some Experiments in Four-Dimensional Vision*[1]. Mr. Claude Bragdon, the translator of Ouspensky's *Tertium Organum*, has provided it with a preface.

I do not propose to describe these experiments in detail. I am less interested, for the purpose immediately in hand, in the details of space-time phenomena than in establishing the fact of the existence of a state, or continuum, in which the reality of all entities exists, and in which it will continue to exist, after the forms in which it is clothed in our three-dimensional world have passed away. For this purpose one of the most striking features of the book is the confirmation it affords of the thesis that the reality behind every natural entity is life, or personality.

Mr. Hodson tells us that:

. . . as soon as clairvoyant sight is "turned on" one becomes aware of extremely potent discharges of energy from the earth itself, from one's own body and that of one's colleagues, as well as from the object [under examination] itself. At first these numerous streams of energy are extremely confusing, and the clairvoyant must in some way develop the technique of self-insulation, both mentally and physically, from their effects. Again, every atom of these emanations and of all solid substances [and therefore of the subject under investigation] contains consciousness as well as energy, and all objects display visibly their whole story to clairvoyant sight.

It would be difficult to find a more exact confirmation of the position taken up in the preceding chapters of this book. Every atom of every solid substance is alive. Exactly. The objects examined with astral sight were, first, a small solid cube, and later, a closed book.

Mr. Hodson examined these objects with closed eyes, and, throughout the experiments, retained normal physical consciousness. He conversed freely with his "examiner", Mr. Horne. Omitting many interesting details, as irrelevant to my present purpose, it may be noted that Mr. Hodson was able to see all the faces of the cube as if each was at the same

[1] Published by Messrs. Rider & Co.

time at right angles to him. He could see them from both within and without. Its lines were in motion, but the motion was such as to be accomplished without moving away from the starting point.

Motion in this manner seemed to take place both inwards and outwards. It is a pity that he did not move the cube about, in order to report the connection between three-dimensional motion and its four-dimensional "reality". He is conscious of the presence and action of tremendous energies and forces within and around the cube. He can see the radiations from it. He can see the play of the molecular and atomic activities within it. This is in fact accomplished at an early stage at which the vision has not become fully "astral". It is a stage known to theosophists as "etheric". I will not pursue this refinement further. The closed book had for him an aura. It gave him a sense of being alive, of being an entity with individuality. It had character. He could read the printing without opening the book.

All this is in full accord with the thesis that we have been developing.

The two experimenters conducted an experiment with time, which consisted in the clairvoyant reporting on his own personality. Here again I will not go into details. It must suffice to say that what he reports on each stage of his life, as he looked back through it all, is precisely the *Linga sharira*—the long man.

At each period he saw himself as the integration of all the preceding years. The whole of his life existed as an integration, which could be pictured at any point at will. He realized that he existed in the future as well as in the past, and reports on that future. This is, in effect, exactly what we have urged. We exist in the realm of reality as the integration of our past.

Further, it is possible for clairvoyant sight to see the three-dimensional facts, corresponding to what the reality was at any given time, as a projection of that reality. It would seem that the shadow continues to co-exist with the substance in some strange fashion. Our past co-exists with our present in both three and four dimensions. What we call time is a dimension of space to the inhabitant of space-time. He can live in four dimensions, while retaining the power of seeing the three-dimensional projection at any point in that space, or, in other words, at any point in what we, in this world, have to call time.

The authors note that the free-will difficulty crops up in a rather novel form on the astral plane. If the clairvoyant can see the future it must be predetermined. To my mind the difficulty, though logically insuperable, is seated in the fact that will, or free will, is a synonym of life, and life is the real existence of every natural entity. Life is, in other words, by definition free will.[1]

For the theosophist space-time is only one of many dimensions. It may be so, but for my present purpose the matter does not seem to require discussion. For the ordinary man it is enough to know that there is a realm of reality, in which all that is not evanescent of him exists, and must continue to exist.

I must now turn to another matter. In a previous chapter I have noted that Professor Whitehead considers that time is something essentially different from space. He comes to this conclusion because, whereas an object can be divided in space, it cannot be divided in time. He holds that time is produced by the recurrences of Nature. He thus concludes that time is, as it were, a function of recurrence. I trust that I am reporting a difficult point in a difficult philosophy correctly, if briefly. He has in this way excluded the space-time of Einstein, and the other orthodox physicists, without supplying a substitute continuum in which reality can exist.

What he has substituted is an alternative mathematical

---

[1] What the clairvoyant presumably "perceives" is the interplay of the wills that are concerned in the physical happenings. If he fails to take account of the volitions concerned he may fail to make an accurate prediction. To give a somewhat childish illustration, a man, who in the best fairy-tale tradition is able to talk to a sheep, tells the animal that he will die next day. He does this because the butcher has told him that he intends to kill the sheep. But what becomes of the prophecy if the butcher dies, or is taken ill? These happenings are also due basically to the interplay of wills—other wills.

explanation of the Michelson-Morley experiment, which creates a diagrammatic space-time consisting in a picture of a volume being drawn through time. Such a space-time has of course no real existence. Each natural entity carries with it a "spatio temporal system" which is the result of its motion relative to all the other entities.

I will not stress the fact that this conception is not verified, either in the mystic experience or in the variety of that experience which is found in clairvoyance, such as that of Mr. Hodson. It is sufficiently obvious without restatement in detail.

Further, it is not accepted by his brother scientists. Finally, it fails to provide the reality behind phenomena, that is to say behind our sensory experience, with a habitation. Such a reality exists for him, and he stresses the fact of its existence with admirable clarity; but he does not answer the question. How does it exist? He recognizes that all experience is on the same footing of reality, and that mental states are as real as physical. This being so, his mental states are as homeless as the physical, neither of them being based on anything. In the upshot the universe, as reported by our minds and senses is the only universe in which we can ever be interested.

I would add that in my opinion, for what it is worth, his conception of time is not essential to the rest of his philosophy. On the contrary, it forms one of the major difficulties which I have experienced in understanding it. Others may have had the same experience. Read with a background of Einsteinian space-time, his metaphysic appears to me to be admirable, and singularly complete. Read, as he would have me read it, it promises nothing but an endless process of increasing complexity, which tends, or may be supposed to tend, to a gradually increasing æsthetic satisfaction for the God who made, and informs, the universe. Assuredly there will be no other intelligence to appreciate the process, since Whitehead provides no continuum in which such an intelligence could continue to survive.

The new outlook, which this book is intended to explain, should be helpful to all those forms of research which, like that of clairvoyant theosophy, depend on the examination of rare faculties and powers. To the materialist the phenomena associated with their exercise savour of the miraculous, and are therefore beyond the scientific pale.

If, however, the view of reality which I have tried to set forth is accepted, it follows, not only that such powers may exist, but that their existence is a necessary consequence of a view of the universe which tells us that miracles may, and must, occur. Where all physical laws are statistical, that is to say are statements of probability, exceptions to their operation *must* take place in varying degrees of likelihood.

When such an exception is reported, and when it is so uncommon as to appear unnatural to certain intelligences, the proper attitude to adopt is that of being guided by the available evidence. The prevailing attitude of sheer disbelief is simply unscientific.

CHAPTER VIII

CONCERNING OUSPENSKY AND HYMAN LEVY

In the previous chapter I have discussed some of the features of the philosophy of Professor A. N. Whitehead, more especially those features which pertain to the problem of space and time. In the present chapter I shall speak mainly of the same problem as treated by P. D. Ouspensky.

His *Tertium Organum* was first translated by Messrs. Bragdon and Bessaraboff while the author's whereabouts were unknown. This was about the middle of the First Great War. A young Russian appeared at the house of Mr. Bragdon, a resident of the United States, and there induced him to co-operate in translating a Russian manuscript. As Mr. Bragdon knew no Russian, and Mr. Bessaraboff little English, the consent of the former must rank as one of the minor miracles. The excellent translation that resulted is another.

In the result, the *Tertium Organum* was published by Mr. Bragdon's private press in 1920, while the whereabouts of the author were still unknown. He was subsequently found among the refugee population of Constantinople, and later, through the kindness of Lady Rothermere, was assisted to come to England, where he wrote his second notable book, entitled *A New Model of the Universe*.

The *Tertium Organum* was a revolution in philosophical thought. It showed that the space-time mathematics of Minkowski and Einstein has a real relevance to the constitution of the universe. Space-time is not only a mathematical assumption that lies behind the physical equations, by which mathematicians have been enabled to calculate the movements of the heavenly bodies with greater accuracy than was possible by the Newtonian method, and which also enters extensively into the modern researches into the microcosm; it is also a fact which has been recognized by the mystics of all the ages, and is the main ingredient of the characteristic state to which they attain. In other words he has established the objective reality of what was previously regarded as a theoretical assumption connected with a strange form of mathematics.

In doing so he has revolutionized our conception of the nature of reality. I have shown in previous chapters that this has enabled us to view the universe as a living reality, founded on living units which inhabit space-time, while the world of sense is, as it were, the shadow, the projection of that reality.

Following Minkowski, he holds that time is an imperfectly understood dimension of space. The fundamental space-time equation for "flat" conditions is capable of being put in a form in which the time co-ordinate is indistinguishable from the space co-ordinates. This must mean that in some manner time is one with space.

By a series of arguments, in which he deals with the forms of consciousness exhibited by various living organisms, such as the snail and the dog, he shows that the lower the organism the more dependent it is on time. Thus time for them is the measure of an ignorance of space which varies with the rank of the organism under consideration. Man has acquired a further power of insight into the nature of space in that, through the concepts of language, he is able to regard as three-dimensional space a number of experiences that the lower organisms can only connect on the thread of time.

Thus, for man, time represents an ignorance of a fourth-space dimension. For animals it represents a further ignor-ance—that of three-dimensional space.

At this point the method is altered, and Ouspensky shows, by a veritable deluge of example and quotation, that the space-time of the physicist and the mystical continuum of the mystic are one. He shows further the essential nature of that continuum. He shows that in it everything is here and now: that everything is alive: that, in short, space-time is a fusion of space and time in which all reality exists.

Space-time is mathematically illogical, and cannot be understood by our reason. The mystic continuum has precisely that nature. I have dealt with all these matters in previous chapters. I refer to them again in this place in order to present a conspectus of the wonderful work that Ouspensky has accomplished.

As a minor reminder of his importance to the modern outlook, I may mention that this book could not have been written without his work as a background.

It is fair to describe a philosopher, who has penetrated to the essence of the reality behind the show of things, and who has shown that that reality is one with the reality visioned by the Hindu philosopher as Nirvana, and by the Christian as the Kingdom of Heaven, as the maker of a philosophical epoch. Had Ouspensky written nothing but the *Tertium Organum* he would be among those few whose writings are "monuments more enduring than bronze".

I am afraid that I must go on to point out that his *New Model* has not, for those who are not mystics of the Yogi type, increased his reputation. By the time he came to write it he had evidently become, to all intents and purposes, a Yogi himself, and a believer in the Hindu religion, considered not only as a philosophy but as a religion based on the dogmas of caste and reincarnation.

Considered as a philosophy, the Hindu religion has given to the world a view of reality which modern science can accept, and which all religions, which are not based on sheer superstition, can and should utilize. Taken, however, as a religion, the Hindu religion is one of the most dogmatic and least useful to mankind which the world has seen.

From this new viewpoint Ouspensky has built up an ingenious structure of argument which is more a piece of special pleading for the truth of the Hindu religion in its crudest form than a genuine contribution to philosophy.

To my mind the most valuable chapter in the *New Model* is that in which he describes his own experience of the mystic continuum. I have dealt with this matter in detail in an earlier chapter. His dissertation on dreams is also of great interest and (possibly) importance. It is based on his own youthful researches into this difficult topic.

For the rest, the book deals with very unfamiliar matters—unfamiliar, that is, to Western thought. He has a long discussion on the superman, who appears to be one with the Master Yogi. Another chapter deals with the occult system of the Tarot. A third with the miraculous, and so on. The real point of the book is, for the Western type of thinker, contained in the chapter which sets forth his New Model: that is to say, his latest view of the real nature of the universe.

He does not profess to base it entirely on facts which are known to science. Indeed he gives us views on matters like the mechanism by which light is propagated, which are avowedly intuitional. To those who are unable to share his intuitions they are hard to understand. Personally, I make no profession of being able to understand them. *Tant pis*, I suppose.

He accepts Einstein's mathematics, that is to say, he accepts the space-time of Einstein as a very "timid" presentation of a matter, which he is prepared to treat more boldly. He considers that time should be treated as a three-dimensional solid, which exists (apparently) side by side with the three dimensions of space. The solid contains not only all the things that have taken place or that will take place in time, it contains also all the things that might have taken place or that will in the future take place in time.

Surfaces cut from this solid contain all the repetitions that take place in Nature. Thus every pulsation of an atom takes place on such a surface. As, in his view, every phenomenon of the universe is repeated, and has been, and will be repeated over and over again, it follows that every phenomenon has such a surface as the locus of its repetitions. He calls this the plane of endurance. But side by side with this uniformity there is a sense in which phenomena repeat themselves inexactly, in which they exhibit variation. This means that, to this extent, they cease to be contained on the surface of endurance, but bore upwards or downwards through the solid in the direction of "eternity".

In addition to these concepts, we are told that the line of time taken by each entity through the time solid is the line of what we call time in the world of three dimensions. This line is invariably curved and ultimately forms a series of loops on the surface of "endurance". When drawn up through the direction of "eternity" the lines become spirals. Hence the time solid must be viewed as a mass of spirals proceeding in every direction.

Personally I find that the conception reminds me of a gigantic mattress stuffed by a lunatic with spiral springs going in all directions. The conception, which is not meant to be derogatory to Ouspensky, may be of assistance to others. Thus every time-line twists and turns upon itself "in many a backward streaming curve." The time-lines go forward and backward, and in every other direction, but always end in forming a series of closed curves on a surface of "endurance". I gather that the closing of such a curve marks the end of one life and the beginning of another. In human affairs it represents the process of reincarnation. As everything is alive, everything goes through an analogous process.

I understand that, for Ouspensky, the atom is a single completed pulsation, after which the entity is "reincarnated". The idea, if I have grasped it, is most puzzling, and, for any-one who is not interested in viewing the world as a mass of mystical repetitions, it appears to be singularly barren. I need hardly say that it is not in any sense proof. Ouspensky tells us that he has in preparation a mathematic of the universe, based on Euclidean concepts, which will take the place of the "timid" Einsteinian mathematics. We must therefore be prepared to suspend judgment. A genius like Ouspensky is capable of any *tour de force*.

He is not afraid to face certain odd results of eternal repetition. He views with equanimity the notion that a man, by being reborn as one of his own ancestors, is in a position to reform his own grandfather by suitable efforts toward enlightenment. I am afraid that Western thought is unprepared for such oddities.

To revert to the time solid, Ouspensky's simile seems to me to raise further difficulties. He believes in Einsteinian space-time, so far as it goes. I infer that he holds the space-time continuum to be to this extent homogeneous. But if there is a time solid co-existent with the space solid, how can the resultant continuum be homogeneous? There are then two continua.

It is, of course, possible to hold that the time of our world is the time that is merged in space to form space-time. It is possible to hold that there is also a "space-time time", which measures a further ignorance and a further adventure in the life to come.

Perhaps, as Ouspensky seems to hold, there is even a third time. Presumably he comes to this conclusion intentionally on the basis of his mystic experience. If, however, the time solid is intended to clarify this notion, then all I can say is that it does not clarify it for me.

I cannot see why I must regard the course of the time-lines as being necessarily curved. Of course, if they are to be regarded as curved, we have arrived at a diagrammatic representation of the endless repetition, which for the Hindu characterizes the universe. Very few Westerners are likely to accept this exotic idea. There are a few who do so, but they are likely to remain few.

Then, the time solid contains a direction of "eternity" which embraces not only all the events that have happened, or will happen, but also all the events that might have happened, or that may happen in the future.

Here again I find myself in a difficulty. In what sense are events, which have never occurred but which remain as mere potentialities, to be described as events at all? I suppose that, for the Hindu philosopher, all possibilities must be realized at some time, and on this assumption they may be held to have a factual element. For those of us who have resisted the temptation to become Hindus the notion is surely fantastic.

Further, since in a four-dimensional continuum there are no forms, no boundaries, and no directions, how is it possible to explain its properties by means of a geometric simile? Such a continuum is as much a state as a continuum, and no one would dream of explaining a state by such means. I have to confess that for me the New Model bristles with difficulties, if it is to be taken as a contribution to metaphysics. If it is intended merely to illustrate the leading ideas of the Hindu religion it ceases to be such a contribution.

I must now turn to Ouspensky's conception of the superman. For him the founders of the great religions are among the supermen. Supermen are on a different plane from ordinary men. They achieve this position by arriving at categories of thought to which ordinary men cannot reach. They are as different from ordinary men as the butterfly is from the chrysalis. I gather then that the Hindu Yogi, who has achieved enlightenment, is either a superman, or else is well on the way to becoming one.

Such a person lives with the idea always before him of the unreal nature of the world of three dimensions, and with the vision of a reality behind it that is impossible to ordinary men. Supermen cannot be simply great business men, great conquerors, or great scientists. Ouspensky tells us that they must be either magicians or saints. The object of the processes of the universe is to produce such men. Christ was one of the greatest of the supermen. Ouspensky pictures him in the likeness of a Hindu Guru giving occult instruction to his *chelas*. It is of the essence of Hinduism that mystic instruction may only be imparted to a select few. It must be kept from the multitude. *Odi profanum vulgus et arceo* might be taken as the leading motto of the Hindu religion.

Ouspensky points out that Christ frequently enjoined his followers "to tell no man". He dwells on the mysticism which underlies many of his utterances, especially utterances such as those contained in the Sermon on the Mount. He considers that Christ has appeared not once, but many times, on earth, and always in the same historical setting. He professes to see that the actors in the Christian drama show signs of having become, through this repetition, letter perfect in their parts.

For the ordinary Christian this kind of thing is pure fantasy. If Christ was the teacher of a secret system of occultism to a small band of persons in whom He discerned mystic possibilities, why is it that, as soon as He passed away, His followers proceeded to found in His name a religion, which has, as its main object, the spreading of His teachings over all the world? Why is the first assumption of Christianity the fitness of every human soul to receive His word? Of course His utterances have a mystic quality; but this does not mean that they were intended to be kept secret. What He insisted on was that every man has this quality. Christians know that through prayer the most cryptic, the most paradoxical, of His utterances become invested with a mystic truth.

It is precisely in this quality of universality that the greatness of the Christian religion declares itself. It brings salvation to the door of every man while the Hindu religion reserves the benefits of "true" religion for a handful of high caste persons.

However, I shall deal with this matter in more detail later. The wastefulness of the Hindu notion is surely, in itself, a condemnation of its cosmic adequacy. There is, apparently, a great Creator at the heart of things, who is pictured under various forms for the unenlightened multitude. Brahma, Shiva, and Vishnu, represent aspects of Him.

If the only result of His operations is to produce endless reincarnations, accompanied by unending pain for the vast majority of His creatures merely in order that a few persons may receive enlightenment, then the game is surely not worth the candle.

If the life of the average Christian is as futile as that of the average Hindu, then, the repeated appearances of a Christ become so many vanities. They accomplish nothing that is worth while, and they accomplish that nothing at great cost. *Parturiunt montes nasciturridic ulus mus*. Ouspensky's superman is that mouse.

The *Tertium Organum* establishes a common-sense metaphysic for common-sense men. It enables them to see that they are, at one and the same time, immortal souls with an immortal destiny, with which they tamper at their peril, and three-dimensional animals living, with the aid of three-dimensional faculties, in a three-dimensional world.

The metaphysic applies to all men, and provides all men with a basic outlook on the universe, that is at once mystical and practical. It is a very great philosophical work—to my mind, the greatest that the world has seen since materialism began to degrade humanity. But, what shall we say of the *New Model*? I have here attempted to provide the reader with the means of answering that question.

At this point I propose to introduce some consideration of materialistic theories, as they are presented by reputed materialists, who write with a competent knowledge of the conclusions of modern science. For this purpose I have selected three men. I am not sure that any of the three with one exception is, or claims to be, a materialist. This is why I stress the qualification that they are materialists by reputation.

Mr. Hyman Levy, the author of *Modern Science* owes a reputation of this kind to a publication called the *Free Thinker*. Shortly after the first chapter of this book appeared in the *Hibbert* I received a copy of the *Free Thinker* with a notice of my paper, and a recommendation to correct my lamentable ignorance of the matters about which I had written by reading Mr. Levy's book. Needless to say the notice was unfavourable. It described my paper as being too ill-formed to merit discussion.

I obtained and read the book and hereby tender my thanks to my adviser; for it is good, very good. I cannot, however, understand why it was recommended to me by an admirer of the *Free Thinker*, for anything further removed from the tied-house type of thinking to which that publication seems to be committed can hardly be imagined.

Mr. Levy is not only a competent, a brilliantly competent, physicist, he is also a scholar and a philosopher. His book is a model of clear and interesting exposition. It is not, however, in any sense materialistic. It accepts the facts which all competent scientists accept and makes practically no further attempt to interpret them philosophically than to hope that some day an interpretation will be found which reconciles their numerous inconsistencies with the ordinary processes of reason?

We have spoken of these inconsistencies several times already and need say no more here than that they relate to the identification of particles with waves, time with space, the vanishing of matter, and so forth. It is hardly necessary to remark in this connection that we have found the reconciliation for which he hopes in the vital theory. I can find nothing in his book that militates against it and, as I shall show presently, he has a striking passage which leads directly to it.

He bases his hope for the emergence of some theory, which will embrace and reconcile all the puzzling aspects of modern science, on the fact that in the past scientific theory has progressed in precisely this way. The men who held that the sun goes round the earth were replaced by men who held that the earth goes round the sun.

Newtonian theories of gravitation, time and space were first supplemented by a plausible, but fictitious, ether, and then by relativistic doctrines which threw them all into the discard. The old-fashioned atom has, similarly, been broken up, and has now dissipated into a mist, through which the bases of our knowledge are discerned as fantastic entities that take Protean and self-contradictory aspects. In this process it will be observed that the wisdom of one era is the foolishness of the era which it supplants.

Mr. Levy holds that we are now on the verge of another generalization, which will once more gather knowledge into a coherent and understandable whole. From this I gather that he is in a fit state of mind to accept our vital theory, which effects precisely the unification he desires.

There is, however, more specific evidence in the same direction; He speaks of Clerk Maxwell's "demon" who was able to defeat the operation of the second law of thermodynamics by operating an ingenious mechanism. Such a creature might conceivably by the aid of this mechanism separate the slow from the fast-moving molecules in a mass of gas; thus re-establishing an order which the law would otherwise operate to defeat. He would, moreover, do this without the expenditure of energy. The process, would replace disorganization by organization.

Mr. Levy very acutely points out that the defeat of the second law is, on this showing, brought about by intelligence. He goes on to say that in actual life men are demons of this kind, who perpetually defeat the tendency of the universe to return to a disordered chaos by organizing its energies in so far as they can reach them. He infers that the second law of thermodynamics does not apply in its totality to a universe that includes human beings.

Precisely. And what if the whole universe is a plenum of living entities each of which possesses intelligence and purpose? To such a universe the second law of thermodynamics has no application whatever. It is the universe contemplated by the vital theory. It appears to be a universe which Mr. Levy could accept without a qualm, scientific or otherwise.

I cannot go on discussing this fascinating book, mainly because it covers much the same ground as that covered by Sir Arthur Eddington's. The latter is more fundamentally philosophic, but the two books move on parallel lines, and, in the connection in which I am now interested, afford no contrasts.

The two following chapters contain more detailed discussions on two other books, each of which may be regarded as describing a modern view of materialism by a writer who is loath to give up that philosophy entirely.

They are at opposite poles from each other and therefore defeat each other. From what I have seen of such writings this failure to find a common basis of agreement appears to be their most prominent characteristic.

CHAPTER IX

THE MIGHTY ATOM OF
PROFESSOR NORTHROP

In preceding chapters of this book I have given reasons for
supposing that the old-fashioned materialism is inconsistent
with any informed view of modern science.

There is, however, a sort of modern positivism, which
accepts the facts that are fatal to materialism, but, none the
less, contrives what may be termed an up-to-date version
of the same doctrine out of them. It seeks to build up a
mechanistic theory of the universe on a basis which is not
mechanical. As Professor Whitehead has wisely remarked
we no longer know what mechanism is. A typical book of
this kind is Professor F. S. C. Northrop's *Science and First
Principles*[1].

The author is well-equipped for writing on his chosen
subject. In addition to being a professional philosopher he
is a competent mathematician. His view of the universe
turns on the theory of relativity, and of that theory he gives
a most able and interesting account. He tells us that it is a
pleasure to expound it; and I can assure him that I have
found it a pleasure to read his admirable exposition. I do
not propose to enter into this topic further than is necessary
to introduce the distinctive turn which Professor Northrop
gives to it.

He points out that the special theory, that is to say the
theory which deals with unaccelerated motion, replaces the
old absolutes of space, time, and the ether by another absolute
called space-time. The general theory deals with the motion
of actual bodies, such as the sun and stars, and that motion is
always accelerated. It carries the conclusion of the special

[1] Published by Messrs. Macmillan

theory a step further, and takes the last remnant of objectivity from space and time.

Northrop goes on to show that the general theory not only deprives space and time of their ancient status; but that it also dethrones space-time and geometry itself. All that remains are the relations of moving masses to a particular mass selected as a reference body.

What Einstein has done is to express the motion of physical objects in a form which remains constant for every shift of the reference body. Professor Northrop holds that Einstein and Whitehead are probably the only two scientists who have grasped the full implications of the general theory. The others write in the manner of "degenerate Hindu mystics" rather than as scientists. I gather that what he means is that the average physicist fails to recognize that, for every change of the reference body, we have a change in the geometry of the region under consideration; and that a change in the geometry implies, and means, a change in the nature of its space-time.

An observer on this planet will invest the sun with a surrounding metric, or curvature, which will differ from the curvature found for it by an intelligence on Sirius. In the result there is no standard way of measuring either space or time, since both change with the region concerned.

Our author considers that this disposes of the reality of space-time also. The only realities he allows to exist are the moving masses themselves. Einstein's relativity is for him too thoroughgoing. By depriving Nature of every kind of standard, or referent, it makes the whole meaningless. If Nature can assume every form, and if all the forms can be true for some observer, then it cannot be said to have any "real" form for any observer. This reduces the human imagination to helplessness.

The universe cannot be either bounded or unbounded; finite or infinite. Einstein in considering the shape of the universe introduces a distinction between space and time. Space can return on itself. Time cannot. He therefore pictures a cylindrical universe in which the direction of the axis is the time dimension. This makes time fundamental. But the rest of his relativity theory assumes that there is no fundamental difference between space and time. Thus Einstein obtains his cylindrical universe at the expense of his fundamental principles.

DeSitter imagines the universe to be spherical, so that time as well as space can return on itself in the space-time merger. This means that his space-time is not completely defined by matter. It thus presents the aspect of an absolute mathematic, and is for this reason rejected by our author.

We then pass with our author to the unitary theory. As all masses are built up out of atoms, and as atoms are focal points of electromagnetic forces, it follows that these forces are at the basis of the universe. They underlie all the phenomena of gravitation and acceleration. It ought therefore to be possible to bring them within the scope of relativity physics. This Einstein has done.

Here a difficulty arises.

The atoms are in motion, but that motion is of a random kind. It ought not to give rise to an orderly universe. The heavenly bodies ought not to exhibit the constancy they do exhibit.

Again, in theory, if each heavenly body produces a different metric in the space around it, we ought not to be able to measure astronomical distances with any approximation to accuracy. Each change of metric changes the length of the rod or light ray, which we use as our standard, as soon as it comes within its influence.

The distance of Sirius from the sun has no meaning if the very nature of the intervening space depends on casual objects about which we know nothing.

But, as a matter of fact, there are many practical reasons for supposing that the metric of astronomical space is reasonably constant.

Hence, what has to be explained is the order, the uniformity of Nature, in despite of a theory which denies the possibility of order or uniformity.

Here Northrop points out that the relativity theory is

defective only because all the factors have not been taken into consideration. There must be some entity which operates to stabilize the otherwise random motions of the atoms. It must also operate to stabilize the metric of the universe. Such an entity would provide a standard, a referent, to which motion can be referred. Further, since every mathematical structure must be ruled out as being inapplicable, the new referent must be physical.

To cut a long story short, our author finds his referent, his stabilizing factor, in a supposed great atom. He calls it the macroscopic atom. This atom encloses the universe so as to prevent any portion of it from escaping. It also exerts a constant stream of force internally, in such a fashion as to create a constant tendency towards uniformity in atomic motions, which would otherwise be wholly random. This atom is spherical. It is also eternal. It is also unchanging.

Whitehead faced the difficulty of accounting for the order in the universe by ascribing it to God. He rests the proof of the existence of God, which we have given in the second chapter, on the existence of this order. Northrop has not improved on Whitehead in this matter, as I propose to show later.

What is chiefly interesting is the fact that modern science must have some explanation of the order in a universe, which ought to be in disorder, if current theory tells the whole story.

For the moment it looks as if DeSitter is justified in his spherical universe of space-time. Perhaps mathematical relations have a greater objective reality than Professor Northrop will admit.

In dealing with the quantum theory our author points out that the inter-relatedness of the universe, in its microscopic aspect, ought to be recognized as fully as the relativity theory recognizes it on the astronomic or macroscopic scale. Radiation determines the motion and behaviour of atoms, but atoms in turn determine the nature and amount of the radiation. "The wave or macroscopic aspect, and the corpuscular aspect are both parts of a single system, and neither can be defined in terms of the other."

Owing to the constant field of force emanating from the great atom, there is a certain amount of order in the universe. Owing to the random motion of its primary particles there is, equally, a certain amount of disorder. The former tends to produce an unchanging universe; the latter a universe in which change is universal and unregulated.

The order that we see in the heavens, and their comparative stability, are due to the great atom; as is also the order that we see in the constitution of the atoms themselves. Thus, the stability of the atom is part of the stability of the universe.

The random electron breaks from one position of comparative stability only to run into another. On this principle the discontinuous nature of energy is supposed to be explained. Further, any moving particle affects its field, and must do so by causing a wave. In this way the apparently illogical and contradictory aspects of the electron receive an explanation. In one aspect the particle is a wave; in another the wave is a particle. I proceed with my summary of an argument which I have increasing difficulty in understanding.

"The jump of an electron, and the propagation of light, are not a serial temporal process; but a reorganization of Nature as a whole." It is from this process of constant reorganization that we get our ideas of space and time. The process is the reality behind all things. Space-time is a fiction of the same kind as space and time. I gather that, as the process of change always takes the same form, the constant velocity of light ceases to be mysterious.

The disorganization of an atom in one place is compensated by the organization of another somewhere else. In all this I am giving as best I can a summary of reasoning which I cannot always follow. I can only trust that my readers will be able to do so.

The existence of the order introduced by the great atom means that the second law of thermodynamics is not completely applicable to the universe. It is fully applicable only to a universe composed of atoms which move in a wholly random fashion. From this point the argument is increasingly difficult to follow. It appears that the great atom somehow operates as God. It does so by being an essential part of a great process of becoming.

A state in that process is the universe we know. It has been produced entirely by the interplay of forces of disorder, represented by the individual atoms, with the force making for order and proceeding in a constant and unvarying volume from the great atom. Everything in such a universe is part of everything else.

This, by the bye, is a singularly mystical pronouncement. It is in full accord with the Hindu philosophical tradition. Professor Northrop would probably be shocked to realize the coincidence.

He gives us some singularly illuminating examples of this cosmic interdependence. Thus the oxygen of the air around us affects the human body in a proportion determined by the pressure under which it is inhaled. But that pressure is a function of physical facts which stretch out to the stars. Thus the human body is dependent for its maintenance on processes which extend throughout the universe.

His general position is that of Whitehead, except that Whitehead substitutes a personal God for the macroscopic atom. It represents a truth, a fundamental truth with which this book is in full agreement. But of the two ways in which that truth may be accounted for, I much prefer that given by Whitehead. I propose to give reasons for this preference later.

Mind and imagination are, in some way, products of the interplay of the forces coming from the great atom with the random activities of the ordinary atoms. I do not follow the reasoning by which this is established; but, I gather that, since all that is assumed to derive from a single process, mind and imagination must be included among its products.

If I am right, Professor Northrop is here making an assumption which is not very informative. Form appears to be due to the fact that the great atom has physical form, and thus gives rise to the forms, not only of the world of sense, but also to those perceived by the mathematician and the artist.

The spiral is prominent in nature because it is a sort of mean between the random rectilinear forms of modern science (I presume the reference is to the movements of the atoms) and the spherical form of the great atom.

I refrain from giving further details of a discussion which at this stage I have ceased to recognize as argument. I therefore pass on to what is, for me, the core of Professor Northrop's book. It lies in the assumption that the stuff of the universe is conscious. The atoms and electrons are conscious, and the great atom is conscious. Each particle of "stuff" has three attributes. It is at one and the same time physical, formal or reasonable, and psychical.

I can only suppose that this means that every electron, every atom, and every combination into which electrons and atoms enter—that is to say all the natural entities—are alive. With this conclusion I of course heartily agree.

Certain physicists are quite unable to get over their ingrained dislike of transcendental interpretations of Nature.

Professor Northrop is clearly of their number. He starts by emphasizing certain shortcomings in Einstein's relativity, and adds his emphatic disbelief in the reality of either space and time, or in the generalization called space-time, which merges space and time. All he sees in Nature at the outset of his book is the operation of *physical* entities on one another. He would mend the deficiencies in the relativity theory by postulating the existence of a *physical* atom, which contains the universe.

Later on he finds that his physical entities have to be understood in a manner that is inconsistent with all previous ideas about what constitutes a "physical" object. It must be conscious, reasonable, and capable of æsthetic and religious appreciations. Had he begun by assuming that his entities have these attributes, he would have wondered why anything in its real aspect need be regarded as physical. The word has no meaning when applied to the ultimates of modern science; but it has a very definite meaning when it is taken as equivalent to life. This is, of course, the sense in which it is taken in this book.

His denial of reality to space and time, and also to space-time, seems, similarly, to be due to an instinctive avoidance of everything that smacks of the transcendental. But does his denial mean anything?

Space and time are for the ordinary man the conditions under which objects exist. For the ordinary relativist, the merger of space and time into space-time is a scientific generalization, which is necessitated by experimental facts.

It is implied in the generalization which has replaced the Newtonian view of gravitation. Some day space-time may be similarly caught up in a wider generalization. But each generalization is true for the knowledge which produced it, and it does not become untrue when further knowledge leads to its replacement. It merely becomes inadequate. But this is not all.

Can we think of anything as being unconditioned? To make this assertion means that we cannot think at all. As water is essential to the wave, as air is essential to breathing, so are space and time essential to all objects of the kind that are loosely termed physical. And if space and time are essential, then the generalization that merges them into space-time is equally essential.

Space and time are the generalizations needed to enable us to understand the existence of form. Space-time enables us to comprehend the fact of bare existence, without assuming form. Nothing can exist without conditions, and conditions cannot exist without an object. Both are real. The one cannot be denied without denying the other.

The relativity theory shows us that form is not inherent in physical objects. This follows from the fact that they change their form with the motion of the observer. At speeds approaching the speed of light the distortion is very marked. The same conclusion seems to emerge from the facts of the quantum theory.

Radiation can be a wave and a particle at one and the same

time. The electron cannot be located either in space or time. What the relativity theory needs, therefore, is a continuum, a background, against which formless, or potentially formless, entities can exist. Space-time supplies just that continuum.

Had Professor Northrop begun by accepting space-time instead of by denying its existence, he would have been led by a train of reasoning to the conclusion which he has actually reached by a process of multiplying assumptions. His failure to do so makes it difficult to understand what he means by his great atom.

We must suppose that it does not exist in space-time; since for him there is no space-time. It must therefore exist in space, and endure through time. But he denies the reality of time and space. It is composed of homogeneous physical units; presumably units like photons and electrons, and sends a constant stream of force through its volume. What force?

Again, I suppose, electrons and photons. But how does it maintain itself under these conditions? If it is continually pumping energy from its shell into its interior, it is continually increasing a pressure that it has to resist, and at the same time reducing its capacity for resisting it. Some time, it ought to blow up. If it keeps exchanging its substance with its contents, its function as a container appears to be rather hard to visualize.

Again, if its stream of force is homogeneous, is this consonant with the fact that the energy which it supplies is capable of operating on all the units which it contains? I cannot see that it is. It must surely supply energy in the varied quanta which are accepted by the various kinds of atoms in its interior. I cannot see how to explain these difficulties. I imagine that most of my readers will find themselves in the same position.

Of course, if Professor Northrop had commenced by accepting space-time, he could never have imagined the great atom. Spheres cannot exist in space-time any more than any other physical form. For him the prime realities, the prime mysteries of the universe, are stuff and motion; or, to put it more shortly, stuff in motion.

This is an unsatisfactory way of attacking the basic problem. It appears to be an artifice for getting rid of space and time, to say nothing of space-time. To the man in the street motion is not mysterious. It is as natural as any other phenomenon. It can be observed and measured and therefore ranks with all other three-dimensional happenings. For the scientist it has its mysterious side, as when he comes to consider how kinetic energy exchanges with the potential variety; but this does not worry the man in the street.

For those who accept the vital theory propounded in this book, motion is the three-dimensional aspect of a mysterious four-dimensional activity, which we can represent to ourselves as the interaction of the lives, which are the reality of every entity, on each other. Moreover science, in the quantum theory, accepts energy in the form of quanta as being four-dimensional.

Our supposition has the advantage of reconciling the three-dimensional world of ordinary experience with a real world of four dimensions in which it has its being. Both are real; but they are realities of different categories.

I have given considerable space to the consideration of Professor Northrop's book, because it illustrates the sort of difficulty experienced by the physicist, who tries to give a coherent account of the universe on physical lines. He must have an absolute frame of reference, but, as will be further noted in the next chapter, physicists do not agree on their physical frames. A frame of reference, an inertial frame, a referent, such are the samples of the terms in which scientists describe what the man in the street calls a background of reality.

We have found it in this book in space-time, regarded as a plenum of the life or lives behind all physical and all natural entities. There may be, I suppose, natural entities which are not, for us, physical. Such a plenum may well perform all the functions attributed to the macroscopic atom by Professor Northrop. It is obvious that it performs the function of explaining the existence of life, consciousness, intelligence and free will far better than that monstrosity. I am sure that, as soon as Professor Northrop gets the better of his coyness about space-time, he will be disposed to accept this opinion.

Balaam was persuaded by an angel (not by an ass) to bless where he came to curse. Professor Northrop is in need of some equally transcendental persuasion.

CHAPTER X

THE DYNAMIC UNIVERSE

I TAKE for the title to this chapter the title of an exceedingly able and suggestive book by a physicist named James Mackaye.

It is a book about physics and not about metaphysics. Nevertheless, some of its implications, possibly most of them, have marked metaphysical bearings. On the one hand, it constitutes an effective and, at the same time, constructive criticism of the Einsteinian theory of relativity. On the other, it seeks to show that there is a fundamental substratum of reality in the physical universe, which the relativity theory in its pure form does not allow for, and which, in the writings of some of its advocates, appears to be denied. In order to get some idea of its scope, let us outline the primary notion at the back of the relativity theory, as propounded by Einstein.

It amounts to this. A fly on a revolving wheel sees the objects around it whirling in all sorts of rapid arcs. For it the sun rises and sets every few seconds, or possibly several times in a second. Objects like trees and houses have the same sort of motion. If the fly considers that it is at rest on the wheel, all these motions will appear to it to be genuine, and a part of the ordinary workings of Nature.

Man is on a wheel of another kind; but one which produces for him effects of the same nature. For him the sun is a small disc which passes across his sky once a day. If he is a primitive man he will accept this as a sufficient description. If he is not, he will have other views.

A man on the sun, in the same manner, would see a totally different set of motions. For him the fly on the wheel and the man on the planet called the earth move in ways which neither of them would recognize as having any relation to what they consider the truth about their movements. They may indeed consider that the truth is that they do not move at all.

The argument can of course be extended, until it is appreciated that all movement is to be regarded as relative. There is no referent, no standard from which motion is to be judged, and from which it can be regarded as having an absolute aspect.

This is the basis of the relativity theory. The great merit of that theory is that it provides a mathematic which can be applied indifferently to all those relative motions. It assumes on the basis of the Michelson-Morley experiment that the fly, the man on the earth, the man on the sun, and the man in any other situation in the universe, will find that the velocity of light is a constant.

The Michelson-Morley experiment necessitates an equation in which length has to be replaced by what is called the interval. The interval is composed of the three space variables together with a fourth variable, which represents time. The four taken together make up the interval, and the interval will be the same for all beings in all situations in the universe.

The original relativity theory dealt only with uniform motion. Later, Einstein extended it so as to include accelerated motion, and with it motion due to what Newtonian physics called gravity. He has since made a further extension, which has the effect of bringing the electro-magnetic field within the scope of relativity mathematics.

It is evident that a mathematic, which deals only with relative motions and energies, deals with a shifting universe in which nothing has an absolute meaning. It has no background of reality. Science depends on measurement, and, if all measures change with the position and motion of the observer, there is no measure which has a permanent meaning. Einstein's mathematics are from this point of view the mathematics of a kaleidoscope.

To this conclusion about the universe there are many objections, apart from the general feeling of practically everybody that it must have some basis, that there must be some sort of fundamental background of reality in Nature.

Mr. Mackaye's book is written round this and other weaknesses in the theory of relativity. It also suggests a possible absolute to which the phenomena of the universe can be referred.

It is to be noted that Professor Northrop's book, which formed the subject of the last chapter, has precisely the same object. He deals with it, as we have seen, by imagining the universe to be enclosed in a vast macroscopic atom with constant properties and exercising a constant field of force on all that comes within its volume.

Mr. Mackaye has gone to the opposite extreme, and pictures an absolute which is composed of points of tremendous radiant energy distributed throughout the universe. What he pictures is in fact a substitute for the ether, which the Michelson-Morley experiment with light failed to detect, at any rate in any form in which it had hitherto been pictured.

Like Northrop, Mackaye considers that space-time is a concept which has no existence, and no meaning. With him this is not an assumption. With Northrop it is. Mackaye bases his rejection of space-time on a rejection of the whole theory of relativity as having a physical meaning.

Unlike Northrop he does attribute physical reality to space and time.

I need hardly point out that this book is in sympathy with both writers to the extent of postulating the necessity for an absolute of some kind. It finds it in life.

Our author has no difficulty in showing that there are physical facts for which the relativity theory cannot account. When its exponents try to do so, they end by contradicting its basic assumptions. As I am not concerned to prove that the relativity theory is a universal explanation of all physical facts, I need not dwell on this aspect of the book at length.

As a sample of the argument I may cite the case of inertia. This is the quality in matter which resists change of motion. Einstein has identified it with gravity; but it turns out that his identification is not absolute. It is not identical with gravitation, but bears a proportion to it.

Mr. Mackaye points out that there are several cases in

which inertia has real physical significance, and that it is not always produced as the relative counterpart to the motion of some other body. The latter contention is that of the relativists.

A man is sitting in a train and is thrown forward when the brakes are suddenly applied. This may be explained on relativity principles, and Einstein has so explained it. Our author points out, however, that the man on the embankment does not undergo a similar experience. On the relativity theory he thinks that he ought to do so.

Rotation, again, such as that of the earth round its axis, presents another aspect of the same difficulty. So that, taking the railway train example as one of linear acceleration, and the example of the spinning earth as one of the rotational kind, it would seem that both kinds of acceleration have a physical reality for which the relativists do not account. The relativists themselves are inclined to cite the total sum of matter in the universe as the cause of both gravitation and inertia. This speculation is the basis of the notion that there are curvatures in space-time in the neighbourhood of matter, and also that there is a world curvature. It is to the presence of the latter that inertial and gravitational effects are ascribed.

Our author, however, points out that such an assumption contradicts the relativity postulate that there is nothing in the universe to which the motion of a material body may be related, except another material body. He seems to have the best of the argument.

In point of fact the relativists are, like the rigid physicists in the opposite camp, looking for an absolute—for a fundamental frame of reference. The former find it in a cosmic curvature, which their theory does not allow them to postulate, while the latter try to find it in other ways, such as those devised by Northrop and Mackaye.

To both the latter there are independent objections, the chief of which appears to be that each of them postulates a physical entity that no one has ever observed, and which no one appears likely ever to observe.

As Mr. Mackaye is careful to point out, even Eddington,

much of whose reasoning appears to infuriate him, makes full acknowledgment of these shortcomings of the relativity theory.

We may conclude that the relativity theory has many shortcomings, and that it is not a universal explanation of macroscopic nature. We may also conclude that the search of the relativists for an absolute frame of reference in Nature has so far failed to yield adequate results.

Mr. Mackaye thinks that the relativity equations are of the nature of a mathematical trick, which substitutes imagined changes in space and time with each new frame of reference, for physical changes which are due to the Doppler effect.

The Doppler effect is not difficult to understand. It means that, when a radiating body is in motion, the radiation in the direction of the motion is crowded together so as to make the wave lengths shorter, while the waves in the opposite direction are correspondingly spaced out and appear longer. The former waves show a shift to the violet and the latter a shift to the red end of the spectrum. They will not be perceived at all from a body which is not in motion relatively to the radiating body.

The suggestion is enticing and ingenious. It very probably has some truth in it. I cannot, however, delay to discuss the matter.

What is of importance to note in connection with the main subject matter of this book is that all modern physicists, to whatever camp they belong, are conscious of an obligation to search for some reality behind physical phenomena, and that they agree in admitting that such reality must exist.

It may, I think, be conceded that the relativity theory deals adequately with gravitational effects in the sense that it enables the paths of some of the heavenly bodies to be calculated to a greater degree of accuracy than was possible under the scheme of Newtonian physics. I imagine that this is only possible in the cases in which the gravitational constant can be supplied *aliunde*. It will also be conceded that the four-dimensional mathematics of that theory are standards of research in the case of microscopic phenomena. They are therefore enormously serviceable, as well as being strikingly original.

I am under the impression that Mr. Mackaye would admit this. What he does not seem to have appreciated is the remarkable manner in which Einstein has deduced his gravitational equations from a general algebraic expression in four variables, on the basis of two assumptions only. One of them is that in regions remote from matter his result must reduce to the equation necessitated by the Michelson-Morley experiment, which deals with uniform motion; the other is that under all changes of co-ordinates the form must remain unchanged.

The transcendentalist may well be excused for seeing something unearthly in this application of pure mathematics to the facts of Nature. It is almost a pity that Mr. Mackaye is not a transcendentalist. He has missed an æsthetic pleasure.

Well, this takes us a step back. We must revert to the basic equation for unaccelerated motion.

If the Michelson-Morley experiment is accepted as correct, and so far it has held its ground without serious question, then it must be admitted that the equation which rests on it is representative of a physical fact. That fact is that if light has the same velocity for all observers, whether they are in motion relative to it or not, then time and space must be regarded as arbitrary divisions of a more fundamental continuum which merges them both.

I will not here restate the reasoning by which this is arrived at. I have given it in the first chapter in a summary which should suffice.

It boils down to saying that the fly on the wheel, the man on the earth, the man on the sun, and the man on a runaway star will each measure the time and space co-ordinates of two given events differently; but all will arrive at the same value for what is known as the interval. This interval is therefore an absolute. It is not strictly a physical absolute, since it relates to a continuum of four dimensions called space-time.

Mr. Mackaye would prefer to call them four variables

rather than four dimensions but I cannot see that this makes any difference to the argument. Moreover, the equation is such as to be capable of being put into a form in which each variable is symmetrical with the others. In other words, the time variable appears in precisely the same form as the variables relating to space, so that they become indistinguishable.

If, therefore, the Michelson-Morley experiment is to be accepted, it seems to follow that every pair of events in the universe is linked by a quantity which is the same for all observers.

Further this quantity exists in a continuum of four dimensions—a fact which necessarily follows from the form of the equation. If the interval exists, the continuum exists; or else the equation is wholly without meaning.

For Mr. Mackaye the continuum is without meaning because, in the first place, he hopes that, in some manner, a physical ether will be restored to science and, secondly, because a four-dimensional entity is not physical for him. I trust that I am not misrepresenting him in thus summarizing what I take to be his views.

It is surely reasonable to suppose that the ether, for which the Michelson-Morley experiment failed to find a basis, was not found simply because it is a four-dimensional entity, and therefore in a category which lies outside the purview of physics. The alternative of denying the existence of all four-dimensional entities leads to the search for a fundamental inertial frame where no one has hitherto found it.

Mr. Mackaye very candidly acknowledges grave difficulties in the way of accepting his dynamic frame. The frame found by Professor Northrop would certainly be rejected by Mr. Mackaye. For aught I know there may be a dozen independent suggestions for supplying a physical frame of reference and, if there are, I am confident that no one of them would be accepted by the authors of the rest.

The reason for this is that physics has come to the stage at which it does not know what a physical frame is. When we come to the ultimate particles of Nature, the electrons, protons, and photons, we are at a loss to say in what manner they exist. The photon is a packet of action, and is accepted to be four-dimensional. Or does Mr. Mackaye accept that description? It is very generally accepted. If the photon is a four-dimensional entity, then why make a difficulty about accepting the only continuum in which such an entity can exist?

The electron and proton, again, cannot be observed with an accuracy which would enable anyone to determine their nature; but it is generally felt that the difficulty of framing a theory as to how these ultimates behave is mainly due to the fact that the kind of continuum in which they exist is in doubt. This can only mean that that continuum may be four-dimensional. It is not an argument against the existence of a four-dimensional continuum to say that it presents illogical features.

Our logic is derived from three-dimensional experience and cannot be expected to apply to a category of Nature which lies outside that experience. In deference to possible susceptibilities, I will not here enlarge on the fact that a large number of persons, known as mystics, claim to have experienced just such a continuum.

With these considerations before us, it is reasonable to hold that the inertial or absolute frame, of which we are all in search, lies in the four-dimensional continuum, and that, in place of an ether, a curvature, a mighty atom, or what not, it is filled with life. Mr. Mackaye supposes that the physical points, in which his inertial frame consists, give off exceedingly powerful radiation.

Well, has it occurred to him that life also is capable of producing remarkable physical effects with an expenditure of energy which is absurdly disproportionate to them? Has he ever beckoned a two hundred pound friend across the street?

If we may assume the existence of space-time we must assume that the mystery called motion has its explanation therein. Or perhaps I should use the word "origin" instead of "explanation". If the ultimate particles of Nature, the electrons, protons and photons are, as I have contended, alive, then the four-dimensional continuum is a plenum of life.

Moreover, our three-dimensional world must be related to the four-dimensional as the shadow is related to the substance. Hence motion may be the shadow, the projection, of the inter-action of these lives on our world. This supposition would account for the mystery attending the interchange of kinetic and potential energy, which our author discusses in a very able and interesting fashion. He considers, to put the matter briefly, that in some manner his ultimate particles (he calls them materions) receive and store the potential energy as it is lost in its visible or kinetic form.

Our four-dimensional plenum of life, that is to say space-time, may just as easily be supposed to fulfill the same function. In my view the very considerable success which has attended the theory of relativity in all its sections is very largely due to the fact that it relies on the element of mysticism known as space-time.

The type of physicist to which, I take it, Mr. Mackaye belongs is resolved to remain within the four corners of what he takes to be the physical. He does not try to explain or account for the many facts of experience which cannot be scientifically observed, and which, therefore, lie outside the range of physics. In other words, physicists of this type avoid becoming metaphysicists. By doing so they lose a great part of their effectiveness as physicists.

This follows from the fact that when science comes down to the ultimate constitution of the universe it meets facts which challenge the validity of human knowledge, and even of human reason. If they stop short at this point, I mean if they refuse to consider all the possibilities which this situation opens up, they are, in effect, refusing to explore any path to knowledge other than that to which they are accustomed. Most of them refuse to admit that there is such a thing as an alternative path.

The matter is even more serious than I have represented, because the scientists to whom I refer allow it to be inferred that their physical outlook on the universe is the only possible outlook. In doing so they must shut their eyes to the side of existence which recognizes pleasures and pains, colours and sounds, æsthetics and religious experience. They are, of course, at liberty to shut their eyes to anything they please; but are they at liberty to encourage the rest of the world to imitate them? I think not.

This, at any rate, appears to be the attitude of the modern successors of the old-fashioned materialist. I trust that, when I say this, when by implication I include a brilliant physicist like Mr. Mackaye in a class which I do not respect, I am not doing him a wrong. After all, my classification depends on nothing more tangible than a general impression of his attitude, as derived from a book which contains no speculation of a transcendental kind.

CHAPTER XI

THE OUTCOME

In this the penultimate chapter of my book I propose to describe the kind of impact which the philosophy that has been set forth in it may be expected to have on human life, when large numbers of men come to believe in it.

The change from the thinking that marked the last century will be so marked as to make men wonder how two such fundamentally different types of thinking could have existed in such close temporal proximity to each other.

The rationalistic outlook of the nineteenth century viewed the universe as a vast lifeless process in which, by some cosmic accident, what we know as life appeared on a microscopic fraction of the sum of things called the earth.

The vital outlook denies that any portion of the universe is dead. It denies that there is anywhere in the sum of things any entity that is not alive, intelligent, and purposeful. From the electron to man everything lives. Outside this earth, under conditions of pressure and temperature which forbid evolution along the line of the carbon compounds, there are in all probability other lines of evolution which our senses are incapable of appreciating. Those lines may be assumed to have given rise to other beings, possibly more wonderful and more intelligent than man.

The universe on this showing is a plenum of life in an enormous number of forms, in possession of senses of which we can make no picture. Indeed, since what we know of form is the outcome of our particular sensory furniture, it can give us no guide to what form may mean for these inhabitants of our universe.

In what we call the lower forms, by which I mean the

chemical combinations that we call inorganic, we assume that the universe is fairly uniform; but when we come to speculate as to what may be constructed out of those primary forms, on the analogy of earthly evolution, we have simply nothing by which to guide our speculations. All that we can be fairly confident about—again on our earthly analogies—is that this planet is exceedingly unlikely to be the only one on which life is not utilized to produce evolution.

If life is everything, in the sense that every entity in the universe is alive, intelligent, and purposeful, we must hold that this earth is not the only speck in the universe on which its possibilities are turned to such account.

Once more: the rationalist of the last century supposed the universe to be what he perceived, his senses being aided by instruments which greatly increased their scope. It is what he sees with his eyes, plus what the telescope reveals, plus an unguessed, but vast residue, which may one day come within the scope of observation. Some men are so constituted as to take pleasure in these somewhat monotonous extensions of what is at bottom the same thing.

What, on this showing, man perceives and what he may suppose himself capable of perceiving in the universe is the illimitable expansion of a sort of charnel house.

The last forty years have changed this outlook. We now know that the universe is not what we perceive it to be. We know that behind everything that we perceive is a reality that exists in a four-dimensional continuum. Of this reality our senses are only constructed to see a part, and then only if the object under consideration possesses features which impinge on the three-dimensional limitations of our senses. We never see anything as it is. What we see are those parts of it which happen to cast a shadow on our three-dimensional continuum.

Moreover, what we see bears no more relation to what is than the shadow bears to the substance. To take a concrete example, which happens to be the fundamental truth of the universe, we cannot see life. We can see the forms and motions of, let us say, our fellow men, and we can infer that they are alive. We can do the same by animals. We can infer living qualities from the conduct of certain organisms.

The last forty years have enabled us to draw the same inference as to inorganic entities. We find, as has been insisted on throughout this book, that we *must* do so for every entity from the protons, photons and electrons up.

The alternative is to maintain the fiction of the existence of dead matter, although, when we have pursued it to the quantic limit, we find that it is no longer matter, but something infinitely individual, and infinitely mysterious, which behaves as if it had life.

To sum up the argument, we can no longer state that we can perceive the universe. What our senses show us is a portion of the universe under a guise that is wholly misleading for any purpose, other than the purposes of our three-dimensional existence.

What science tells us of the universe is that it is a four-dimensional plenum of entities, which have no form that we can identify as form, and no motion that we can identify as motion. The entities have some attribute which projects as form, and some attributes that project as motion on our world of three-dimensions. That is all we, as scientists, can say about them.

The mystics tell us a good deal more. They tell us that in that plenum everything is alive, intelligent and purposive. It now turns out that this information is in precise accord with quantum physics and may be accepted as scientific truth. We have indeed travelled a long way from the scientific dogmatisms of the last century.

The next matter which arises in this connection is that of the meaning, if any, that must now be attached to death.

We may grant that the primary forms of life, the protons, photons and electrons are probably deathless. But what are we to say about the superimposed personalities? To take a simple, but typical, example of what I mean, is the personality which informs the radium atom something which must be supposed to survive the explosion that is the death of the atom as an atom of radium?

It will be realized that I am approaching the matter of human survival by stages.

Although we cannot dogmatize about what happens to personalities so far removed from the human, we can at least note that the destruction of any personality is wasteful. If, as we have seen, the universe in its real aspect is a plenum of life, that is to say, of personalities—there being literally nothing in existence which is not alive—then the destruction of any life, of any personality, is akin to a breach of the law of conservation of energy.

The primary energies, exemplified by the protons, photons and electrons, are living personalities, and it will be conceded that there is no difficulty about supposing that they are undying. Why then should the higher flowers of energy, exemplified for our present purpose by the radium atom, have a different destiny?

The question appears to be unanswerable.

The old argument, that when an organism dies it must suffer annihilation because there is nowhere for it to go to, may have had some force in the days when space-time was unheard of. It has, however, no force now. Relativity has provided a disembodied personality of whatever rank with a possible and probable habitat. It is moreover a habitat which our senses are not constructed to penetrate.

Every personality that is based on other personalities, like our radium atom, has energies and powers which are different in kind from those of its constituents. If the various vibrants which make up the atom—the electrons and simple protons (as in the hydrogen atom) are taken singly, no scientific ingenuity will suffice to extract from them the capacities and energies which reside in the complete atom. Atoms, all atoms, have powers which are not possessed by their constituents.

I need not continue an argument, which does little more than stress the obvious fact that every complex personality has powers and energies that are more than the sum of its constituents, in as much as it raises the forces exhibited by the latter to a higher level.

I infer that the higher the personality the greater the cosmic waste involved in the supposition that it is ever annihilated. The assumption that waste takes place in any part of the universe is, presumably, unscientific.

These general considerations may serve to introduce the subject of the survival of our human personalities.

Most of the arguments in favour of this, the only form of survival that has interest for us, have been touched on in the course of this book. For example, we have seen that, in certain circumstances, human beings have experienced a detachment of their personality from the body. This has taken place in some instances at what is evidently a dividing line between life and death.

Men have literally come back from what, to all intents and purposes, was death. A few, a very few, have been able to describe the experience. They do so in terms which are clearly identical with the accounts of the mystics. We have seen, also, that in certain African tribes there are medicine men who have the power of sending their personalities abroad to great distances for the purpose of bringing back news from places which are quite inaccessible to their bodies.

I will not stop to repeat these matters in detail; I recall them merely to emphasize that, under certain conditions, the personality is separable from the body. Moreover, when such separation takes place, the personality generally has an experience, which is irreconcilable with the limitations set by time and space to its activities, while it functions in and with the body.

A further matter to be noted in this connection is that, during this experience, the personality is able to avail itself of something equivalent to sense perception. Thus, the medicine man, who reports an occurrence which takes place several hundred miles away, describes the scene, and the people, of whom he brings report, as if he had seen them by ordinary vision.

Another queer fact, which generally, though not always, marks the mystic experience, is that the separation of the personality from the body takes place while the functions of the body are at their lowest ebb. The Hindu Yogi, for example, usually obtains it when his bodily functions are so completely inhibited as to resemble death. To take another less reputable example, the drug taker obtains his insight while his body is more or less inhibited from acting in a normal fashion, owing to the action of the substance which he has taken into it.

All this amounts to saying that the capacity of the personality for functioning apart from the body rests on a great mass of human evidence. That evidence, moreover, being that of men separated by time, space, race and language, cannot possibly be collusive.

Finally, we have seen in the chapter dealing with Ouspensky's experience, and elsewhere, that the content of the mystic revelation cannot be described in human language. It relates to a continuum of a higher order than ours. We have already noted that the human reason, being based on three-dimensional experience, is not equipped to deal with a further dimension or dimensions. All this rests, I repeat, on human evidence of the most conclusive kind, and it should be noted that that evidence does not in any way conflict with the conclusions or requirements of science.

On the contrary, by establishing the existence of a higher continuum, it supports the general requirements of the relativity, and quantum theories. The relativity theory requires a fundamental four-dimensional continuum, which it calls space-time. The mystic experience describes such a continuum. The quantum theory has to describe quantic phenomena in the language of paradox. The mystic vision perceives a state or condition in which nothing can be described otherwise than in terms of paradox.

There are logical objections to the doctrine of survival, which have a force that is undeniable.

Death seems to occur in a senselessly haphazard manner. Why, for example, do infants die? Why are promising

lives cut off in youth? Why, for that matter, does anyone die while in full possession of ripe faculties, before
he has been able to place them fully at the disposal of
society?

Many a man, who has suffered from an apparently
cruel and senseless bereavement, or who has reflected on
the cosmic processes which produce such events in what
may be termed an insane profusion, has concluded, either
that there is no Divine guidance in the universe, or else
that, if there is a God, He is not entitled to the respect of his
creatures.

The only answer that I can see to this argument is that it
assumes the impossibility of mystical compensations. It
assumes that nothing can conceivably compensate for the
waste and cruelty that go on around us. Why should there
be any waste, any cruelty, in a universe that is run by an
omnipotent and kindly power? From a certain point of view
these questions are unanswerable. If the shadows are all that
there is, the indictment is complete. But, if the shadows are
no more than shadows cast by a mystical and eternal reality,
what then?

Well, there is still no answer, other than that the mystic's
outlook leaves room for hope. For the convinced mystic,
and for everyone who is assured of the truth of the Christian
religion, that hope is sure and certain. It is the fact round
which life centres itself. For the ordinary man, whose faith
has not attained to this mystic certitude, but who believes
that the changes in favour of survival vastly outweigh those
against it, the hope may not be capable of being described in
the magnificent words of the Christian burial service; but
none the less, it may remain as a light to guide his feet in his
journey through life. It has a pragmatic quality, which, as
William James so powerfully insists, is the mark *par excellence*
of mystic truth.

Then we have what may be termed the medical argument.
It denies the possibility of a separation of the personality
from the body, and insists on its dependence on the body.
Senile decay may, and often does, overtake the most vigorous

personality, and reduces it to a spectacle which arouses pity, but never respect.

A glandular excess of deficiency may completely alter a man's character; and it often happens that, when the abnormal physical condition is adjusted by suitable medical treatment, normality is restored. A blow or other accident may have similar effects and be capable of similar cure. In short, if mental states are the product of bodily states, then, when the body disintegrates, nothing that possesses mentality can remain.

Here again we have an argument to which there appears to be no logical answer. It would seem that "the children of this world are (indeed) wiser in their generation than the children of light".

We have of course a number of facts which, if accepted, indicate that the mystical experience is often achieved when the body is in a highly abnormal condition; as when a Yogi compasses it after inhibiting nearly all the functions of his body. Yet his intellectual and emotional faculties, as we have seen, are then at a higher level than was possible to him in normal waking life.

We also have abundant evidence, to which repeated reference has been made, to the effect that the personality can be detached from the body and, as it were, despatched to gather news of events that take place at distances at which the ordinary sense cannot function.

On our vital philosophy the fact that the logical medical arguments appear to be inconsistent with the mystical facts does not require us to choose between them. They may be both true. They are both true. But one set of facts relates to three-dimensional experience: the other to four-dimensional. They co-exist in the realm of reality, and in that realm are reconciled in a manner which logic cannot follow.

An ellipse can be cut from a cone, and projects, or may be projected, into a circle, which is also contained by the cone, yet a circle is not the same thing as an ellipse. I give the simile for what it is worth. Like all similes it must not be carried too far.

With this very inadequate discussion of important matters I now pass to consider how the vital philosophy affects the well-worn topic of human will, or free will.

The old-fashioned argument, which regards the will as a product of the mechanism that produced the rest of the universe, has no relevance to a universe which, in its three-dimensional aspect, has been produced by vital causes. If the texture of the universe is life, then mechanism is ruled out.

Further, since mechanism depends on the uniformities which we call the laws of Nature, and since we have found that these uniformities exist only in the form of averages, akin to those which we make in the social sciences, we are left with a picture of the universe which is based on infinite diversity, rather than on infinitely large classifications which postulate resemblance. Our language is a process of classification, based on the postulate of resemblance, and logic, which is an intellectual refinement of language, emphasizes this position.

They have enormous relevance to our three-dimensional existence. They are indeed essentials to its maintenance, and development at levels above those attainable by the animals. This must not, however, be allowed to blind us to the fact that classification is only possible when we shut our eyes to the phenomena which are inconsistent with it.

On the side of physical science those phenomena have only been generally manifest in the last forty years. Up to the end of the last century our senses lacked the instruments which have since enabled us to realize that, beneath the apparent uniformities, lies a universe of what we must call individualism. We once thought that all elements of a given element were alike. Then, with the discovery of isotopes, we discovered that this is not necessarily correct.

Later, we found that atoms react diversely to bombardment in a manner which arbitrarily endows some of them with radio-activity of as many grades as there are grades of possible bombardment, and that each grade represents the advent of a new, if short-lived, element. In other words there are constitutional differences between the atoms, which can be compared with the constitutional differences we find among human beings.

Thus the whole face of speculation on its scientific side has changed, and we must now replace our assumptions about fundamental uniformities by the assumption of fundamental diversity. Everything in the universe is individual, and everything is alive. Variation is, indeed, the most common mark of the presence of life.

If we regard the ultimate vibrants as simple personalities —they are simple to us—we find that their combinations give rise to higher personalities based on them, such as the atoms, the molecules, and the crystals. The process continues with the creation of ever more complex personalities, until, along the line marked out by the carbon compounds in our planet, we begin a process of evolution which ends in man. In other words we may assume that analogous processes have taken place, and have resulted in the creation of other orders of being, which are not dependent on the carbon compounds.

Now every entity has, as we have seen earlier in this book, certain characteristics, which describe life, and which do not fit into any description of what has been called, without justification, dead matter.

They are, to name only a few, consciousness, purpose or will, and intelligence. It is through the impulsion of these, and other vital characteristics, that the universe as we know it has arisen. As I see the process, each electron can choose whether it will co-operate in making an atom or not. Each atom has a similar choice in directing its activities; and so on all along the line till we arrive at man.

If this picture is reasonably correct, we must hold that each entity in the universe, however humble, is essential to its texture. Its choice to act or not to act in a certain way is a vital factor, which, as time goes on, leads to increasing divergences from a pattern that might otherwise have come into existence. These divergences, moreover, become more and more marked.

Let us now translate these considerations to the only case

which for us has relevance; I mean to the case of man and his responsibility.

Life is something like the mazes that Georgian gardeners used to set up in the grounds entrusted to their care. Each one of us is constantly presented with alternative routes, in the form of choices of conduct; and every choice affects the position attained at the end of a given period of time. We all remember what might have been had we chosen a different calling, or a different wife. Nay, most of us can recall trivial, or seemingly trivial, choices, which have entirely altered the direction of our lives.

Life thus seems in retrospect to have been the resultant of a number of choices great and small.

In the physical maze of the gardener the only issue at stake is the wanderer's position. No moral issue is involved. In the maze of life, however, the moral issue is all important. The man who keeps trying to take the direction which he believes to be morally incumbent on him is improving his quality as an eternal factor in the universe. He is contributing to its purpose, in so far as he is capable of discerning it; and also, it may be, beyond the limits of his discernment.

On the other hand, the man who does not keep trying invariably finds that he is degrading the quality of his personality, and helping to defeat that purpose. Both men occasionally act out of character. The tryer may, he very often does, take the worse course, though he knows it for what it is. The apparent wastrel may on occasion rise to heights, which, judging from his previous life, we should never have expected him to attain. I do not think that any man can be judged by his fellows, except to the extent that judgment is forced upon them by considerations of prudence. We must hate the sin, while we try to love the sinner. Each one of us has to make the best of the talents entrusted to him, and his cosmic value is, we trust, assessed rather by what he has tried to do, than by what he has done.

I once heard a drug addict described as one whom the Almighty had placed in the front line trench of life. However, it is not my purpose to write a sermon. What I am trying to lead up to is the mysterious importance of our choices, and of the quality of life to which they cumulatively give rise.

The maze of life differs from the physical maze in that it is acted upon by every contacting life, even while acting on it. Each choice we make alters the quality of the maze, as well as our own quality. The universe is different for the passage of each one of us through life; and it is eternally different. We alter each other's lives, while we are engaged in altering our own.

If we are trying to be good, we are influencing more people than we know in the same direction; without, as a rule, being aware of our influence. If, on the contrary, we are living recklessly, or carelessly, we may be, we probably are, doing harm, which is far more widespread than we dream.

There are some persons who seem to delight in doing evil, and in leading others to follow their example. I imagine that they belong to the number of whom it was once said "it were better for him that a millstone were tied about his neck and that he were cast into the sea".

We seem to be living in a world in which our every conscious act has enormous significance. Mercifully, in view of the weakness of human nature, it seems that no act is irretrievable. No sinner is beyond redemption provided that he is prepared to try again.

> *"Unhappy man: and why art thou despairing!*
> *God will forgive thee all but thy despair."*

Well, when we are all convinced of the mystic importance of human life, of our responsibility for the lives around us, of the fact of our survival into a state which emphasizes our worth, and our worthlessness alike, with unerring certitude, we will find ourselves living in a better world.

It will certainly be a refreshing change to find ourselves living in a world in which every man, who is ordinarily prudent, will take into consideration the fact that he *must* survive death, whether he likes the prospect or not. He will not like it, if he has not tried so to live that he is not afraid to die.

I have pointed out more than once that the main object of this book is practical. Had the vital philosophy not had a practical bearing on human conduct, it would not have been worthwhile to write it. But, as human conduct depends to a very considerable extent on religious belief, it would seem to be logical to indicate the belief or beliefs which are most consistent with it.

Of course anyone who has read the earlier chapters of this book is aware that the writer is, or tries to be, a Christian. Now, the Christian has suffered, and still suffers, from the grave disability of not possessing a metaphysic. There is no distinctively Christian description of the universe (unless we except that given in the first chapter of Genesis). It would seem that Christians, considered as philosophers, may follow almost any school of thought. They may be followers of Spinoza, Hume, Kant or Hegel. They may be materialists or transcendentalists.

The *credo quia impossibile* form of faith is very common among those whose scientific opinions are at variance with their religious convictions. This is especially true among those Christians who have adopted the scientific views of the last century on the subject of free will and its relation to natural law in a mechanical universe.

The fact is that the characteristic Christian doctrines now stand on the same footing as the modern scientific doctrines. Both have to be expressed in the only manner in which mystical truth can be expressed; that is to say in the language of paradox. The paradoxes of the Sermon on the Mount are matched by such scientific pronouncements as those which express the identity of space and time, the identity of waves and particles, the supersensory nature of the universe and so forth.

The Christian knows that his paradoxes are pragmatically true. That is to say, he knows that they are practical guides to a well-ordered life, and to the comfort of communion with his God. The scientist is in much the same position. His paradoxes are essential also to the development of his knowledge of what he loosely terms the physical universe. They are essential also to the limitations, which he is now compelled to place to that universe. Sir Arthur Eddington has brought out this point admirably in his *Philosophy of Modern Science*.

The universe belongs to a higher order of thought than the human reason can compass. It belongs to a four-dimensional continuum, which is infinitely greater than the three-dimensional section of it with which our senses and our instruments deal.

The Christian religion is, of course, far from being the only religion which rests on mystical truth. It is indeed probable that every religion has this basis. It would seem that most, if not all, religions derive from a perception of the mystical element.

From the African medicine man to the Yogi is a long cry; but each depends for the characteristic quality, which singles him out from among his fellows, on his recognition of it.

What really singles out the Christian religion from all other religions is the fact that, whereas the medicine man and the Yogi regard their spiritual perception as a mark of spiritual superiority, the Christian religion proceeds on a diametrically opposite principle.

The medicine man and the Yogi treat their mystical attainments as a monopoly, which is jealously guarded from the intrusion of the vulgar mass of mankind. Incidentally, it is a very useful monopoly, considered in terms of worldly comfort, and wordly esteem. The prime Christian doctrine is, however, that all men have a right to share in spiritual truth.

To the Christian every human being is capable of being a fellow Christian, and it is his duty to help him to become a Christian. It is on this singular foundation that democracy rests; and democracy has no other secure foundation. This is why democracy can hardly exist in the totalitarian countries and it is worthy of note that Christianity has suffered its most intolerant persecutions in precisely those countries.

The most prominent argument for Christianity in our time is that it is essential to the maintenance of the civilization that is based on it.

The weakness of that civilization is precisely the very serious extent to which it has become diluted and divided by spiritual substitutes and outright denials of the efficacy of the Christian faith.

The denials we have dealt with. The substitutes present a more subtle class of problem. Their basic weakness is, often, that they are treated as equivalents for the Christian faith, when they are not inconsistent with it.

Thus physical health is of importance to the Christian as well as to the Christian Scientist; but to the Christian it is incidental to the business of living, while to the Christian Scientist it is the whole business of living. Both the Christian and the Christian Scientist can agree that our mental attitude towards diease is of enormous importance. They can agree that the mind has notable power over the body in healing, and in preventing diseased conditions. They cannot, however, agree that the exercise of this power is the be all and end all of life. If it were, the Christian Science teachers, and healers, would become members of a spiritual aristocracy, and all spiritual aristocracies are anathema to the Christian.

The western devotees of Yogism present a very similar problem. They seek quietude of mind, combined with bodily health. Both are supposed to result from exercises— generally bodily exercies—based on those prescribed for the Hindu candidate for the mystic experience.

These exercises achieve their object in many cases, and often, to a notable degree. But, are mental quietude and bodily health the only achievements that make life worth living? They will not save civilization. What they will do, in the unlikely event of their becoming a predominant fashion, is to found yet another spiritual aristocracy.

Christianity sometimes achieves one, or both, of these

ideals. But, if it does, the result is incidental. Its cosmic value transcends either, and the cosmic value is the real value, which relegates all earthly values to their three-dimensional insignificance.

Then, let us consider spiritualism. Here we have something which purports to satisfy a genuinely mystic longing, the longing for immortality. It has its points. It has its truths. But the kind of shade that is called up by its mediums is too often of the kind which in Plato's vision "fled gibbering". It is generally unworthy of the spirit it purports to represent. It is always unworthy of the high cosmic purpose that is an integral part of the Christian vision.

The fact that the Christian entertains this vision is good mystical proof of its superior reality, and good ground for his rejection of spurious imitations. The spiritualistic imitation may often represent an imposition practised by powers of darkness, which, as far as the medium is concerned, is believed to be genuine.

If the future of the human soul is what the spirits so often represent it to be, then it fails to fulfill our Christian expectations. This, I think, applies even to the ambitious though wholly well-intentioned descriptions of the afterlife, which we owe to certain mediums, more especially to those whose communications take the form of automatic writing.

I may be unfair to these worthy persons. I do not impugn their good faith; but, I do feel that their revelation is distinctly below the Christian level. In some cases this may be due to the impossibility of describing purely mystic knowledge in human language. It must be beyond human capacity to describe to the human animal his condition, when he ceases to be an animal.

Anyhow, even at its highest, spiritualism does not add to man's capacity for maintaining a Christian society against the atheistic and pagan powers that now threaten its existence. In so far as it diverts men's attention from Christianity it weakens the force of Christianity. In so far as it purports to add to the message of Christianity, it too often degrades it.

To my mind it always degrades it by (even in its most spiritual manifestations) translating into material terms mystic facts, which are incapable of such description. While writing these lines I am reminded of the gorgeous imagery of *Revelation*, and of the vision of St. Paul. The reminder warns me against a dogmatism that I may have expressed too absolutely.

At this point I am reminded that what I desire to emphasize is that modern science, translated into the vital philosophy with which this book deals, supplies a perfect metaphysical background for Christianity. It thereby supplies, as I have previously stated, an essential element which Christianity has hitherto lacked. The lack was not felt during the ages of faith when the mystical, the incommensurable, facts of life were naïvely accepted on the same level as its physical facts.

Shortly before the renaissance, however, the Church began to interpret physical facts in terms of religious doctrine, in a way which laid it open to scientific criticism of increasing power. In trying to maintain this type of doctrine it condemned itself to a losing fight on this side of its teaching, and the exposure of this weakness operated to undermine faith in older and more essential teachings.

That weakness clearly consisted, in the main, in failure to provide its adherents with a description, a philosophy, of the universe, which could resist attack from the side of physical science, and the philosophies, which derive their inspiration from scientific theory.

Christianity, like all other religions, bases itself on a mysticism, which has always had enormous strength from its inherent human appeal, but which, until recently, could be rejected by science as something which is inconsistent with human reason. Reason was the final arbiter for the scientist, and many religious persons were inclined to agree with him.

In the result we had a deadlock. On the one side stood the Christian believer, who marched under the *quia impossible* banner. He was often, indeed generally, the Christian who did not concern himself with the philosophy of either side. On the other stood the scientist with his robust faith in reasoning from the physical facts, as being the only facts with which man has to concern himself. They apparently left no room for mystical faith.

In the last forty years we have seen mysticism invade the domain of science, and the fight, that had been for so many years disastrous to Christian and other forms of faith, turn against the aggressors. A good many of the latter still try to maintain the material ground that appeared so solid until, through the work of the relativists and the quantic physicists, it was seen to be based on foundations as mystic, and therefore as immaterial, as religion itself.

I have given two specimens of their efforts. They are of the nature of *tours de force* of the same kind as the explanations of the universe given by the old schoolmen. I fancy that few scientists are convinced by them, or by any of the comparable efforts which have been made to save science for materialism. Science is now just as much a mystic adventure as the Christian life, and for the same reason.

That reason is that the basis of all things, whether material or immaterial, is mystical. Both science and religion deal with the same all-pervading mystery—the mystery of life. Science deals with it in all its forms, whether organic or inorganic. Religion deals with it in its human aspect only. Both sides admit, or should admit, that the unknown and unknowable facts enormously exceed those which are known or knowable.

The universe is vaster than man's possible knowledge of it by at least a whole dimension. There may, of course, be more than one dimension contained in the unknown. In this book I have dealt with the unknown as being comprised within one extra dimension merely for the sake of simplicity.

We have reiterated *ad nauseam* that the commensurable facts are those which are contained in our three dimensions, and that all the other facts are four-dimensional, and therefore incommensurable. This compels us to recognize that the fundamental structure of the universe is incommensurable. This is merely to repeat that it is mystical.

In so far as religion deals with the incommensurable facts it rests on far wider foundations than science. Its present weakness is that it has largely forgotten the sources of its strength. It has tried to make the best of both worlds, and, in doing so, has forgotten that one of them is as unreal as a shadow.

Having come to the end of a rather sketchy defence of the Christian religion on what I take to be modern lines, someone may be moved to ask what is the Christian religion of which I have been talking. It is admittedly and unfortunately divided into a great number of sects, which in varying degrees are incompatible. It may be urged that, until this difficulty can be overcome, there is small hope of the general body of those who profess and call themselves Christians co-operating for any purpose.

There is an unfortunate amount of truth in this contention. It may be that all sects will learn from the tragic events of our time to lay increasing stress on the Christian elements which unite them. If they can fix their mind on a God who so loved the world that He gave His only begotten Son to die for it, they will make progress in the work of reunion.

I venture to think that, the mystic outlook, based both on the mystic tradition and on modern science, will in certain respects make the task easier.

I need hardly say that my thought in this matter is set forth with the greatest diffidence, seeing that I have no claim whatever to theological learning. It does, however, seem likely that the difficulties and divisions, which are based on human logic, may to some extent yield to the solvent of a philosophy that is based on a denial of the efficiency of human logic in the realm of ultimate reality. I take it that the theologians will consent to start with me from the assumption that ultimate reality is the reality with which we are concerned.

Well, greatly daring, let us commence with the question of transubstantiation. The Roman view, and that of the High Church division of the Reformed Church is that the elements at the Mass, Eucharist, or Communion—to give it the various appellations which are commonly used in the various sections of the Church from High to Low—are changed by the blessing of the officiating priest into the actual body and blood of our Lord.

Below this line we come to the churches which do not believe in a physical change, which to them savours of magic. Their communicants and Clergy regard the ceremony of Communion, as they are wont to call it, as a ceremony of remembrance that Christ died for them, and of thanksgiving for that great sacrifice.

Are the two positions irreconcilable? They are irreconcilable in logic; but in the mystic realm of reality with which religion concerns itself logic has no validity. May not the Roman and High churches be using human words to describe a miracle of spiritual comfort and spiritual healing, which is beyond the power of human language? In attempting such a description they are compelled to have recourse to words which, while they convey, as they are meant to do, the sense of a gracious and loving miracle, nevertheless appear to some Christians to go beyond the proper functions of language.

Surely it is not impossible that Christians who take the latter view, and who do not profess to regard the ceremony as more than an enjoined act of remembrance, also achieve and receive a spiritual benefit of not inferior value. Both are earnestly striving to obtain the greatest possible measure of oneness with the Triune God.

May it not be that the benefit depends rather on the degree of the earnestness with which each communicant approaches the altar, than on the words in which he may elect to describe the nature, and function, of the ceremony?

May not the difference arise mainly from the fact that while one class of worshippers attempts a verbal description of the ineffable, the other refuses to make the attempt?

I repeat that I do not offer this suggestion with the idea of giving instruction to professed theologians. I state it because it arises naturally from the philosophy with which this book is concerned. To its readers it will be apparent that it

proceeds on lines which have been applied to other fundamental matters of Christian doctrine, in earlier chapters.
However, I do not propose to venture further in a direction
in which my qualifications for giving instructions are so
meagre.

I used to wonder why the scientific truths of the last century
should be so uniformly directed against everything that gives
quality to human life. The scientists of that time were honest,
and often both great and good men. Yet, whenever they
touched on the human side of things they seemed to make it
their business to show that human life is merely animal life,
and that all life is of the nature of a cosmic accident in a
universe, which is preponderantly dead, and which in a short
time will be entirely dead.

To quote a phrase, whose author I have forgotten, they
regarded man as a bewildered ape. It appalled me to think
that this verdict might be true. I was even more appalled
to reflect that this terrible conclusion should result from the
application of so much earnestly directed human energy and
human intelligence.

We now see that it was but a passing phase. It may seem
rather terrible that the Creator should, as it were, have
permitted such misdirection of His human family; but such
reflections can be multiplied without much advantage. When
we see the substance, of which all that we now know is a
shadow, we may be in a position to explain these matters.

What I am now concerned with is to point out that the
honest endeavour of the scientists has at the long last justified
itself spiritually as well as materially. It has helped to lead
us out of the valley of the shadows, in which it so recently
seemed determined to keep us wandering. Scientific endeavour, like all human endeavour which is honestly directed,
has spiritual quality, and science now reflects that quality.
It has received, perhaps I should say it has achieved, a revelation of priceless value to a troubled generation. It has found
a unity with mystical experience, which enables us to interpret
human life and the universe from a new angle. And yet the
new angle is not new.

On the side of religion it is as old as Christianity. On the side of philosophy it goes still further back to the earliest Greek thought. What is news is the restoration, the recreation, of an intellectual atmosphere in which the ancient truths can be recognized as truths. We are once more allowed to think mystically as well as physically.

For this priceless privilege we are primarily indebted to science. No honest human endeavour is lost though its fruits often seem slow in ripening. Green fruit is generally bitter.

CHAPTER XII

THE LOOM OF A PLAN

I PROPOSE in this chapter to give a general outline of the view of the universe, which has been discussed in the preceding chapters from various aspects.

They picture a universe in which life is the basis of everything. The phenomenal universe, with which our senses present us, is merely one of a possible infinity of such universes. Life, in the forms in which it is commonly recognized on earth, is associated with sense organs of various kinds. In some cases, as in that of the body cells, we cannot describe them, though their presence may, and must, be assumed. The universe produced for the cell by its sensory apparatus must be something totally different from the universe with which our senses have familiarized us. The difference is presumably less marked in the cases of organizms which have some senses analogous to our own; but it is always present. In fact we may sum up by saying that the universe, as it appears to man, is not the universe that appears to any other organizm.

When we pass from this planet into the outer spaces, we find that the chemical constitution of the heavenly bodies is analogous to that of the earth. At this stage the entities concerned are, as we have argued in considerable detail, alive, conscious, purposive, and intelligent. They are, in other words, personalities.

We may assume that in the outer spaces they have also given rise to more advanced personalities, with senses adapted to enable them to deal with the phenomenal worlds which they construct. These higher personalities will not have been developed along the line of the carbon compounds, as has happened on earth; but along some line, or lines, which enable them to withstand conditions of temperature and pressure that would be fatal to life on earth. Each and all of them may be supposed to inhabit phenomenal universes, each of which is the product of the sensory apparatus of the entity considered, and each of which differs from all other phenomenal universes.

Thus, every entity in the universe, considered as the owner of a sensory apparatus, uses that apparatus to construct its own phenomenal universe, and to maintain its phenomenal existence in it. In this way we arrive at the concept of an infinity of phenomenal universes; but only one "real" universe —the universe of life, considered apart from its physical trappings. To put the matter more concisely, the universe of life is the one and only real universe; but it has produced an infinity of physical universes. No single one of the latter has a reality, other than that implied by its relation to the sensory furniture of the entities for which it exists.

We know that the living entities, which we observe on this planet, cease to possess that furniture when they undergo the change which we call death. It is suggested that all entities, whether by our standards they are regarded as alive or dead, undergo this change at some time. An atom of iron may seem to us to be immortal; but this may only be because its life appears to be infinite by comparison with ours.

The physical is a sort of fantasy attached to the fact of life.

In an earlier place we have shown that the physical only makes its appearance when the stage is reached at which the super-physical entities are massed, to an extent which brings them within the scope of our senses. Till that stage is reached they are super-physical. After it is reached they are still super-physical, but also observable, and therefore physical. I need not remind my readers that the super-physical is to be identified with life.

When we have arrived at the conception that the universe is a plenum of life, which proliferates into an infinity of physical lives, each endowed by its sensory apparatus with a phenomenal universe peculiar to itself, and each enduring physically while its association with the senses endures, we reach a broad principle of cosmic unity of the utmost significance.

Nor does it end here. Our reason is based on language and sensory experience. Both language and reason have been evolved to enable us to deal with our physical surroundings. Beyond those surroundings both are meaningless. When we carry our vision beyond the limits of the human, we catch a glimpse of a similar relation governing life, wherever it exists in association with a sensory universe. We must suppose that every such life has developed a type of reason analogous to human reason, and that it has some means of communicating with its fellows.

To every such life or personality the same limitations as to the scope of reason and language would presumably attach. The basic type of reason is for us inductive. It is the aspect of reason which enables us to marshal our sensory experience. It is common to all men, in greater or lesser degree. It may be assumed with great confidence that it is shared by every entity in the universe, as soon as that entity becomes possessed of a sensory make-up, and thus acquires a physical existence.

The above conclusions fit into the scientific scheme of space-time, as it arises from the results of the Michelson-Morley experiment. Space-time in its most general, and therefore its most fundamental sense, is the continuum in which space and time are merged, and lose their separate identities. It is a matrix from which intelligences, operating on the human plan, separate out their several combinations of space and time, each in accordance with its motion. All intelligences that are in motion with regard to each other will disagree on all locations in space and time. They will, however, agree in finding the same value for the interval.

It thus appears that all intelligences, however situated, have a common measure of happenings, which in some fashion denotes their degree of separateness. As the measure is four-dimensional, three-dimensional intelligences cannot wholly grasp its meaning. They can, however, grasp the fact that it is super-physical,

Science has thus come to the point of recognizing the possibility of a diversity of creatures—an infinite diversity with a common outlook on the super-physical reality from which they all proceed.

Moreover, that basic reality must be, in some fashion, a maximum or minimum condition arising out of the primary space-time equation. It must therefore be the condition in which the observer has a velocity equal to the constant velocity of light. The only observer who is capable of dwelling in this continuum must, one would think, be the Creator. In the term light I of course include the electro-magnetic disturbances which are not visible.

The sum total of the electro-magnetic energy of the universe is, presumably, its physical basis. It is the physical aspect of the super-physical fact, which informs and produces all the phenomenal universes. In its physical aspect it is energy in its various manifestations. In its super-physical aspect, it is life in all its manifestations. In this aspect it is the basic truth behind every entity. This scientific approach to God may be shared by myriads of other entities in the universe, on the showing of our argument.

Incidental to it is another matter of some importance. Men have differed among themselves over the question of whether God is immanent or transcendent. On the vital view, which we have been explaining, He is apparently both. The difference implied by the words is logical, and for this reason appears to be irreconcilable. But our logic does not carry beyond three dimensions, and must be supplemented by some form of mystical insight. The Creator may be both immanent and transcendent in the mystical continuum. The fact that our minds are not constructed to picture the possibility is irrelevant. The Christian religion accepts this position, as will be immediately apparent to readers of St. Paul.

When we look a little more closely into the nature of super-physical reality, we find that the fact that it is super-physical denies it any physical content. The commensurable facts with which science is concerned have no counterpart in it. We cannot locate anything in space-time. What we know as motion must in space-time correspond to a wholly mysterious activity, which can neither be measured nor observed.

Of course every intelligence, which, like ours, divides the fundamental continuum into space and time divisions, will have physical equivalents for location and motion, though they may not agree with ours, otherwise than in the combination known as the interval.

The facts of the super-physical must therefore be incommensurable facts. Life is such a fact and, as we have seen earlier, life has a number of synonyms such as personality, consciousness, intelligence, purpose, emotion. There may be many others. We may take it that these are the facts of the superphysical existence. The commensurable facts are the evanescent facts. The eternal facts are the incommensurables, which give meaning, quality, and individuality to life, but which lie beyond the reach of physical observation.

They all have æsthetic or moral implications. From this point of view, which Professor Whitehead has powerfully emphasized, the æsthetic element in the universe is the fundamental element. Professor Whitehead regards morals as a branch of æsthetics.

Modern science has found room for this position in its insistence that modern physical laws are statistical, and do not profess to deal with the individual particles. It has gone further; since, as we have shown in earlier chapters, there is a great deal of evidence to show that, not only the primary particles, but also all the entities which are dealt with by our chemists and physicists show the phenomena of variation, and show them in vast abundance.

I need here only refer the reader to previous discussions on isotopes, and on the inferences necessitated by the results of particle bombardment. The latter show that atoms of the same substance vary in much the same way as human beings vary in their liability to disease. Some atoms become radio-active under bombardment, while others resist its attack just as some human beings succumb to an epidemic disease while others escape. In each case we must assume the presence of constitutional variations which account for immunity or liability, but which are not capable of being observed in advance.

Now æsthetic or moral quality is essentially individual. Artistic and moral responsibility attaches, and can only attach to individual artists and moralists.

In previous chapters these facts of variation were used to support my argument in favour of the view that the apparently inanimate entities of the universe are alive. Here it is relevant to support the further assertion that, considered as individuals, such entities, in addition to being alive, have, or may have, æsthetic and moral faculties. If they have any attributes they must be of this order, since they cannot have commensurable attributes. It is moreover gratuitous to suppose that they have no attributes, or none that we can conceive of.

It is significant that an independent line of approach has led substantially to the same conclusion as Professor Whitehead.

It is at times difficult to speak of the super-physical without conveying the implication that I am speaking of something that is not likely to be encountered till death has released our personalities into a super-physical universe. The super-physical is the physical; with the understanding that it is the physical only because the units, of which the entity under discussion is composed, have massed sufficiently to become perceptible to our senses.

Everything is super-physical, and remains super-physical after it has acquired the additional attribute of being perceptible. You and I are super-physical here and now. When death supervenes we will continue to be what we are, while disappearing from the physical stage. What we will encounter when we come face to face with the naked forces of four-dimensional reality is unknown to us, except in the mystic reports, of which some account has been given in an earlier chapter. The experience will presumably vary with the desert of the subject. He will get what he has earned.

INDEX

[171   ]

INDEX